Killer Burger Recipes

101 Burgers

by

Thomas Inch

Killer Burger Recipes
101 Burgers

ISBN 978-0-934523-14-1

Editor@Middle-Coast-Publishing.com

Cover Photo Credit
Prayitno
(https://commons.wikimedia.org/wiki/File:A_party_tray_of_sliders_at_a_restaurant.jpg),
A party tray of sliders at a restaurant",
https://creativecommons.org/licenses/by/2.0/legalcode

Back cover insert
Evan-Amos
https://commons.wikimedia.org/wiki/File:NYC-Diner-Bacon-Cheeseburger.jpg, NYC-
Diner-Bacon-Cheeseburger" public domain
https://commons.wikimedia.org/wiki/Template:PD-self

MIDDLE
COAST
PUBLISHING

"Good books are where we find our dreams."

DEDICATION

This book is dedicated to Saint Lorenzo, martyr and patron saint of Chefs.
Pray to him and maybe he will find someone for you to cook for.

ACKNOWLEDGMENT

"It requires a certain kind of mind to see beauty in a hamburger bun." Ray Kroc - founder of the McDonald's restaurant chain.

Recipes

How to Make a Killer Burger

Defining the Essence of a Burger

Hamburgers are an integral part of American culture. In the United States, we eat more than 14 billion hamburgers a year. That calculates out to 38.3 million burgers a day, or 443 burgers devoured every second. A hamburger (burger for short), typically considered a sandwich, consists of one or more cooked patties of ground meat placed inside a sliced bread roll or bun. The patty may be pan-fried, grilled, smoked, or flame-broiled.

The Beef

For this book, when we say the word burger, we specifically mean a beefburger. Not ground turkey, ground pork, or a slice of chicken served on a bun.

While the quality of the ground beef matters big time, the most important variable is its fat content. Simply put, construct burgers from meat that is at least 20 percent fat. Flavor equals fat.

The most common grind of beef used for making a hamburger is ground chuck. It's the popular choice because of its rich flavor and balance of meat-to-fat ratio. That said, specialty shops sell custom blends for hamburgers by adding brisket, short-rib, or even tenderloin to the mix. One very nice blend is a mix of ground prime rib, brisket, skirt steak, and tenderloin, or there's the less exotic mix of chuck and sirloin. It's good practice to experiment with different blends and cuts of meat. But restated for emphasis, the most important variable in ground beef is its ratio of meat to fat.

Exactly What Is Ground Beef?

Food laws define the specific categories of ground beef and what it can contain. For example, in the United States, if the meat is ground and packaged at a USDA-inspected plant, beef fat may be added to hamburger but not to ground beef. In the U.S., a maximum of 30% fat by weight is allowed in either hamburger or ground beef. While in France, the allowable amount ranges from 5 to 20%, with 15% used by most food chains. In Germany, regular ground beef may contain up to 15% fat, while the special Tatar for steak tartare may contain less than 5% fat. Both hamburger and ground beef can have added seasoning, phosphate, extenders, or binders added. But no additional water is permitted.

We prefer a ratio of 80-percent meat to 20-percent fat in our test kitchen, a moist and flavorful mix. Know that aficionados avoid supermarket blends marked lean, generally mixed in a ratio of 90 percent meat to 10-percent fat. A 90/10 lean blend makes a dry hamburger. Conversely, blends with more than 20-percent fat content make for a burger that's loose and fatty. Tip: Add milk and mix to blend if the burger mixture does not hold together when squeezed.

Similarly, avoid off-the-shelf supermarket chuck. Instead, ask the butcher to coarse grind a pound or two of meat. The reason is as simple as the sea is salt. Off the shelf supermarket chuck is ground fine, resulting in a drier, denser texture that is less satisfying to the taste buds. Further, it's best to avoid frozen meat because flavorful juices are lost during defrosting. And don't make the rookie mistake of forming patties before cooking. Instead, leave the ground meat in the refrigerator until ready to cook.

Seemingly a direct contradiction of what we just said, when grilling, consider placing patties in the freezer for 30 minutes before cooking. The reason is as simple as the sea is salt: Patties hold together better when they go on the grill cold, and 30 minutes is too short of a time to do them any damage.

When making burgers patties ahead of time, cover with plastic wrap & refrigerate for no more than a day. Take care to handle the meat as little as possible – the more it's worked, the tougher it gets. Don't press a patty with a spatula, prick with a fork, or frequently turn as precious juices will be lost.

State of Doneness

The degree of doneness measures how thoroughly cooked a burger is, based on Color, Juiciness, and Internal Temperature. Gradations include Rare, Medium Rare, Medium, Medium Well, and Well Done. It's also important to know the interior of a burger continues to increase some 5- to 10°F after having been removed from heat.

Term	Description	Internal Temperature
Black and Blue	Seared black on the outside, ice cold, raw center.	70 F
Extra-rare	Very red - Hot on the outside, raw on the inside	115–120°F
Rare	Red center - Soft	125–130°F
Medium rare	Warm, red center - Firmer	130–140°F
Medium	Pink and firm	140–150°F
Medium well	Hot pink in center	150–155°F
Well done	Gray-brown throughout - Firm	160°F

Overcooked	Blackened throughout - Hard	160°F+

As a burger cooks, its color transition from red to pink, to gray, to brown, and finally, if burned, to a blackened char. Well done cuts, in addition to being brown, are drier and contain few or no juices. Contrary to popular opinion, searing does not seal in juice. That said, browning contributes mightily to flavor and texture.

Also, a burger should be allowed to rest after cooking and before being served. The reason for this exercise in patience is as simple as the sea is salt. Determine the degree of doneness by taking the internal temperature with an instant-read thermometer inserted precisely into the center of the burger poked in at a 45-degree angle. No worries, the small hole won't lose juices.

From your days on this earth, you already know that the basic hamburger falls into two distinct categories: The traditional griddled hamburger of diners and fast food takeout places and the diner-style.

The diner-style patty is thin and mashed flat on the grill and features a burnished crust. The pub- or tavern-style hamburger is just the opposite: Large, plump, and juicy.

Remember early on when we said that to our way of thinking, a burger was ground beef? A worthy exception is ground buffalo, more particularity, American bison. Bison buffalo burgers have less cholesterol, less fat, and boast fewer calories than beef hamburgers. So no big surprise, the American Heart Association recommends buffalo burgers as more heart-healthy than beef.

Greasy Spoon Diner Style Burger

The diner-style hamburger weighs 3- to 4-ounces precooked. Smashed burgers can only be cooked on a flat surface, like a cast-iron skillet or griddle, and not on a BBQ grill

The method is as old and established as the burger itself. Add a tablespoonful of oil or butter to a large cast-iron or stainless-steel skillet and place over medium heat. For each burger, form the ground beef into a ball that's about 2 inches tall.

Put the balls into the skillet with plenty of distance separating them. Use a stiff metal spatula without slots. Smash each ball flat, forming a thin patty measuring about 4 inches in diameter and about ½ inch thick. For more even cooking, make the patties thinner at the center than the edges. Season with salt and pepper

Let cook without moving until the patty shows a deep, burnished crust. It takes about 90 seconds. Then slide your spatula under the patty and flip it over. Add a slice of cheese. Continue cooking the hamburger for about a minute or so longer. Place on a bun.

Pub/Tavern Style

Tavern Style hamburgers are notoriously large. Thick and juicy, their char transitions to tender, medium-rare meat. Like all burgers, it's best cooked in a cast-iron pan, although it translates well on the BBQ grill.

Typically the pub or tavern-style burger's precooked weight ranges from 6- to 8-ounces. Any burger heavier than that is difficult to cook completely through without burning the surface.

Begin by forming a patty one inch thick and 3 ½ inches in diameter to look like a flattened meatball. Minimally handle the meat. Do not pack it tightly. Use just enough pressure, so the patty just holds together. Indent the top of each patty with your thumb. To help it cook more evenly.

Cook undisturbed for three minutes, then flip over. If making a cheeseburger, now is the time to lay on a slice. A medium-rare burger is done in three to four minutes. Remove from the skillet and let it rest for five minutes to fix the flavors.

You Need A Cast Iron Skillet

Invest in a cast-iron skillet. Not an enameled cast iron (Le Creuset), just a plain-vanilla cast iron skillet like the ones commonly made by Lodge. As sure as the sea is salt, there is no better surface to cook a hamburger. As the patty cooks, the fat renders out of the meat, pooling around the patty, crisping, and adding a great deal of flavor. Even better, cast iron cookware adds trace amounts of iron to a diet, and well-seasoned cast iron boasts a nonstick cooking surface that doesn't require additional oils, making it a heart-healthy way to prepare food.

On a BBQ Grill

A BBQ grill is a worthy option. Begin with a hot fire. Cook burgers with the lid up. Don't form patties too loose or too large. Flip them several times to crisp the exterior and cook them thoroughly throughout. Resist the temptation to press down on the patty with a spatula, a rookie mistake that squirts juice and fat on the fire, causing the flames to flare up and the burger to lose precious flavor and burn its exterior. If the burger is cooking too quickly, then use the cooler sides of the grill to rest them.

Tip: While still cooking away merrily on the grill, brush the burgers with butter so that the natural sugars caramelize, making the meat extra-delicious. Lowering the grill top towards the finale helps cheese melt more quickly.

A Word About Cheese

A frustrating happenstance when cooking a burger is the unintentional overcooking of a juicy patty while waiting for its slice of cheese to melt. Some cheese resists melting, especially the good stuff like a Gruyere or an extra sharp cheddar, which is the reason why savvy cooks reach for melts-in-a-flash American cheese, shredded cheese, or grated. Grated cheese with the greatest surface area of the three melts the fastest.

While shredded and grated cheeses melt more quickly than a slice with their greater surface area, there's an issue that may or may not bother. Off-the-shelf, shredded cheese is coated with powder to keep it from clumping in the bag. And while the label says that it's powdered cellulose, more specifically, it's powdered wood pulp. In its defense, cellulose helps stabilize food, lowers fat content, and increases fiber. Benefits notwithstanding, if the notion of cellulose in cheese is an issue, then just stop buying shredded cheese. Instead, buy cheese by the block and shred or grate on the kitchen counter.

The Bun and Condiments

You already know how it's common practice to serve burgers on Brioche buns, English muffins, sesame-seeded hamburger buns, or plain, toasted bread. Or even the ubiquitous potato flour bun for the way it lends a soft, sturdy platform to the patty.

Aficionados also know that a bun is not just a bun, that the under-appreciated hamburger bun has many requirements. It should overhang the edges of the patty and boast a nice flavor that's not so strong to overpower the beef's flavor. Even more importantly, a bun must be firm enough in hand to hold together when condiments and burger grease attack. Conversely, it must be soft enough so that burger juices don't squeeze out when the burger is bitten into, and at the same time, it must hold together, so all of the fixns' (sic) don't fall out. Nobody wants a burger that disintegrates halfway through their meal.

A fresh grocery store hamburger bun will suffice. But there are better options than a mere cold roll fresh from the refrigerator. First, spiff it up with a. 20-second stint in the microwave to render the bun flavor-fully warm and soft.

And then there's toasting.

Toasting a bun activates what's food scientists call the Maillard reaction, a chemical reaction between amino acids and sugars that lends browned food its distinctive flavor as well as firming its surface, so it's easier to spread on toppings. The best-tasting toasted buns are soft on the outside and crispy but not dry on the inside.

One method is to melt two tablespoons of butter per bun. Soften the butter for 10 or 20 seconds in the microwave so that it spreads easily. Or, simply take the butter out of the refrigerator for about 1 hour before you plan to toast the buns. A noteworthy variation on the theme is to mix chopped garlic, or garlic powder, with the melted butter.

Paint the cut sides of the buns with butter to the edges. Place the buns with their cut-

and-buttered sides up on a baking pan so dripping butter. Toast buns in a frying pan or on a pancake griddle (before cooking the meat) for about 1 minute until golden brown and the butter is bubbling. Check the buns about every 5 or 10 seconds to minimize the chance of their burning too dark.

Nota bene: - Lay a slice of lettuce on the bottom bun, under the burger, to protect the bun from becoming saturated with grease.

Burgundy Burgers

Ingredients
1 ½ lbs ground beef
¼ cup Burgundy wine, or ¼ cup red wine
¼ cup finely chopped onion
1 tablespoon Worcestershire sauce
1 teaspoon seasoning salt
¼ teaspoon pepper
1/8 teaspoon garlic salt

Directions
Mix all of the ingredients together
Shape the mixture into six patties, each about ¾ of an inch thick
Broil, or grill, the patties four inches from the heat
Turn once, to the desired doneness, about 10 to 15 minutes
Serve on toasted buns with a favorite topping

Horseradish Burgers

Ingredients
2 lbs ground beef
2 Tblsps steak sauce
3⁄4 teaspoon seasoning salt
1 package (3 ounces) softened cream cheese
1 to 2 tablespoon prepared horseradish,
1 teaspoon prepared mustard
8 hamburger buns, split

Directions
In a bowl combine beef, steak sauce and salt
Mix well
Shape into 16 patties
Combine cream cheese, horseradish and mustard
Spoon about 1 Tblsp of the mixture into the center the patties
Top with the remaining patties
Press them together along their edges
Seal the edges
Grill, uncovered over medium-heat for 10 minutes on each side
Serve on buns

Spanish Burger

Ingredients
1 ½ lbs ground chuck
Salt
Freshly ground black pepper
4 Manchego cheese cubes chunked 1 x ½ x ½ - inch
4 slices Serrano ham or prosciutto
1 tablespoon olive oil

Directions
Preheat grill on high
Arrange the ground chuck in a single layer
Season with salt and pepper
Divide chuck into four portions
Wrap each piece of Manchego in a 4-inch square piece of ham
Heat the cooking oil in a frying pan over medium heat
Add each ham and cheese bundle
Fry, turning, until the ham is crisp and the cheese begins to melt
Allow to cool slightly
Fold meat around each bundle
Form hamburgers about one-inch thick
Grill burgers for about 4 to 5 minutes per side

Mexican Hamburger

Ingredients
1 lb beef, ground
1 package (1 ¼ ounce) taco seasoning mix
1 can (4 ounce) green chile peppers, chopped, drained
1 small onion, finely chopped

Directions
Mix ground beef, taco seasoning mix, green chilies, finely chopped onion
Shape into patties and grill
Serve with salsa

Saucy Hamburgers

Ingredients

1 egg
¼ cup sour cream
¼ cup dry breadcrumbs
¼ teaspoon dried parsley flakes
¼ teaspoon thyme
¼ teaspoon salt
¼ teaspoon pepper
1 lb ground beef
1 cup ketchup
¼ cup packed brown sugar
2 teaspoons prepared mustard
1 teaspoon Worcestershire sauce
4 hamburger buns

Directions

Combine egg, sour cream, breadcrumbs, parsley flakes, thyme, salt, and pepper
Crumble beef and add to the mixture
Mix well
Shape into 4 patties
Combine the ketchup, brown sugar, prepared mustard and Worcestershire sauce
Grill patties, uncovered over medium-high heat for 3 minutes on each side
Brush with sauce
Grill 4 to 6 minutes longer, basting and turning several times, until juices run clear
Serve on buns

Caribbean Grilled Burger
With Pineapple Sauce

Ingredients
3/4 lb pineapple, cored
1 jalapeño pepper, split and seeded (wear gloves)
1 tablespoon molasses
1 lb lean ground sirloin, formed into 4 patties
4 Tblsps island jerk seasoning
1 ½ cups iceberg lettuce, shredded
¼ mango, peeled, seeded, cut in thin, match-like sticks
4 mini sweet red peppers, sliced in rings
4 Kaiser rolls

Directions
Preheat grill on high 10 minutes
Coat grill grate lightly with vegetable oil
Puree pineapple, jalapeño and molasses in a blender
Set aside
Coat the beef patties with jerk seasoning
Sear the burger on grill, about 2 minutes
Turn and sear the other side
Turn meat back over
Reduce heat to Medium or Low
Close lid
Cook burgers to an internal temp of 160 degrees
Remove from grill
Place on roll
Top with sauce, lettuce, mango, and red bell pepper rings

Jalapeño Cream Cheese Stuffed Hamburgers

Ingredients
1 large jalapeño pepper, seeded and finely chopped
16 Tblsp cream cheese, softened (8-ounce package cream cheese)
2 lbs ground beef
1 package (2 ¼ ounce) dry onion soup mix
2 Tblsp fresh minced garlic
8 hamburger buns, split

Directions
Oil the grill grates
Set grill to medium heat
Stir together the softened cream cheese with jalapeño pepper
In a bowl combine the ground beef with onion soup mix and garlic
Add seasonings: Egg, breadcrumbs, Worcestershire sauce
Divide into 16 equal portions
Pat out each portion to a 1/3-of an inch thickness
Spoon 2 Tblsp of the cream cheese into the center of the 8 patties
Do not spread the mixture
Top with remaining patties
Press down along the edges to seal the meat
Grill for about 10 minutes per side or until well done
Serve on buns with favorite condiments.

Nota bene: There is no need to add salt to the ground beef because the dry onion soup already has plenty.

Nota bene: Don't press down on the burgers while cooking or the cheese will ooze out.

Spicy Burger

Ingredients
3/4 cup ketchup
¼ cup Frank's RedHot sauce
1 lb ground beef
1 slice of Jarslberg cheese

Directions
Combine ketchup with Frank's RedHot sauce
Mix beef with ¼ cup spicy ketchup
Shape meat into 4 burger patties
Broil or grill burgers until done
Top with remaining spicy ketchup

Platte County Fair Kraut Burgers

Ingredients

1 lb ground chuck
1 cup sauerkraut, drained
3 hamburger buns
McCormick's Montreal Brand steak seasoning

Directions

Divide the ground chuck into thirds
Then divide each third into half
Flatten into 6 patties
Place 1/3 cup sauerkraut on each of the 3 patties
Top with the other 3 patties
Seal around the edges
Sprinkle with steak seasoning
Grill until done
Place each burger on a bun
Top with mustard or your favorite topping.

Note bene: Platte County, Missouri, USA is renowned for its kraut burgers.

Teriyaki Burgers

Ingredients
1 lb ground beef
1 egg, beaten
¼ cup teriyaki marinade, sauce
¼ cup finely shredded carrot
1 can (3 ounces) French-fried onions
4 slices Swiss cheese
4 onion hamburger buns, split

Directions
Preheat grill to high heat.
Mix all ingredients together, except for Swiss cheese and buns
Form into 4 patties.
Grill patties 5 minutes on each side
Top with cheese
Serve on buns

Homemade Hamburgers

Ingredients

1 lb lean ground beef
1 medium onion, peeled
1 medium potato, peeled
2 eggs
½-1 cup breadcrumbs, or 2 to 3 slices of bread, torn into small pieces
Salt and pepper

Directions

Grate the potato and then the onion in a large bowl
Add one of the eggs and mix with spoon
Add salt and pepper
Add the beef and the other egg
Mix until well blended
Add breadcrumbs until the mixture sticks together but is not too dry
Add salt and pepper
Shape mixture into 4 patties, each one about ¾-inch thick
BBQ, fry or broil the burgers for 10 to 15 minutes

Herb-Garlic Butter Hamburgers on a Grill

Ingredients

3 Tblsp finely chopped mixed fresh herbs: Parsley, basil, oregano, chives, tarragon
1 garlic clove, minced
½ cup salted butter, softened
1 ½ lbs ground sirloin, ground round, or ground chuck
Coarse salt
Black pepper
6 deli hamburger buns

Directions

Place all of the herbs, garlic, pepper, and butter in a small mixing bowl
Beat with a wooden spoon until slightly fluffy
Place a 12 inch square piece of plastic wrap or parchment paper on the work surface
Mound the flavored butter in the center.
Roll the herb butter into cylindrical shape
Twist the ends of the plastic
Compress the butter
Chill the butter in the refrigerator, or freezer, until firm

(To make the hamburger patties)
Unwrap formed butter and cut crosswise into ¼" to ½" discs
Form hamburger patty fully around one butter disc
Press gently, sealing the disc in the center of the meat
Place burgers on hot grill
Grill burgers until done, about 5 to 7 minutes per side (medium-done)
Add cheese
Set aside for about 5 minutes, in order to allow flavors to fully meld
Brush buns with melted butter and toast on the grill for a few seconds
Serve with condiments of your choosing

Nota Bene: The herb butter keeps for up to 5 days in the refrigerator, or up to 3 months in the freezer

Juicy Hamburgers

Ingredients
Salt and pepper
2 Tblsp ice water
1 lb ground chuck
2 to 3 crushed ice cubes

Directions
Dissolve salt and pepper in ice water (at least ½ teaspoon of salt per pound of meat)
Add spiced water to the meat, then add crushed ice and work in gently.
Form 4 patties
Grill or pan fry

Nota bene: An old sausage maker's technique, dissolving salt and pepper in ice water distributes spices more evenly throughout the meat

Peanut Butter Burgers

Ingredients
4 large hamburger buns or 4 large rolls
2 lbs hamburger
¼ cup creamy peanut butter
2 teaspoons minced garlic
2 Tblsp finely chopped onions, or 2 Tblsp thinly sliced onions
4 Tblsp honey barbecue sauce, more if desired
4 slices white American cheese
4 slices lean bacon, cooked, more if desired
4 slices tomatoes
2 cups prepared creamy coleslaw
4 teaspoons spicy mustard

Directions
In large bowl, combine hamburger, peanut butter, garlic and finely chopped onion
Shape into four patties
Sprinkle both sides with salt and pepper
Place on hot grill and grill until almost done
Turn once, cooking about 3 minutes per side
Spread the top of each burger with half of the BBQ sauce
Turn
Top opposite side with remaining BBQ sauce.
Grill for 1 minute, turn burgers again.
Top each burger with cheese.
Grill another minute longer, or until cheese has begun to melt
Toast the buns
Place burgers on bottom buns
Split the bacon slices in half
Top each burger with 2 half slices of bacon
Spread inside of top buns with spicy mustard and place on top of slaw

Hamburgers with Brown Gravy

Ingredients
2 lbs ground beef
6 pieces potato bread or white bread broken into small bits
1 envelope onion soup mix, dry. Salt to taste
½ teaspoon pepper
2 Tblsp ketchup
½ teaspoon garlic powder
2 teaspoons parsley flakes
2 eggs
2 envelopes brown gravy mix
2 cups water

Directions
Combine all ingredients in a large bowl until well mixed
With approximately 1/3 cup of meat mixture form patties about ½ inch thick
Heat a 12" skillet over medium-high heat
Fry burgers for about 5 minutes on each side, until they're almost done
Remove burgers
Plate
Discard all but about a tablespoonful of drippings from skillet
Lower the heat under skillet and prepare brown gravy with water in a bowl
Slowly pour into skillet, stirring constantly, scraping any brown bits from the bottom
Once the gravy has thickened, replace burgers in the pan and cover
Simmer for about 20 minutes, or until burgers are done
Serve with mashed potatoes or egg noodles

Stuffed Pizza Burger
(Combination Pizza and Burger)

Ingredients

1 lb ground beef
2 teaspoons black pepper, freshly ground
2 Tblsp garlic powder
8 ounces sharp cheddar cheese, coarsely shredded
1 lb pepperoni
8 ounces pizza sauce (of your choice)
8 hamburger buns
1 lettuce head (optional)
1 tomatoes (optional)
¼ cup pizza sauce

Directions

Combine, hamburger salt and pepper in a large bowl
In another bowl, combine the coarsely shredded sharp cheddar and pepperoni
Let bacon and cheese mixture sit at room temperature for about 20 minutes to soften
Shape mixture into balls
Form 2 patties of meat and place one cheese/pepperoni balls in between them
Pinch the sides together in order to seal in the cheese ball
Gently press formed patty
Spread the cheese ball
Continue until all patties are formed
Grill burgers on a medium flame for about 7 minutes on each side
Flip the burgers and baste the cooked side of the patties with the pizza sauce
After 7 minutes the burger should be done
Baste again with the pizza sauce before removing from grill
Butter hamburger buns and place on top rack of grill for several minutes, until toasted
Build the burger with tomato or lettuce

Nota bene: Big burgers take longer to grill.

Barbecue Burgers

Ingredients

1 ¼ lbs lean ground beef
2 to 3 Tblsp barbecue sauce (use a rich flavor not a sweet one)
1 bag barbecue potato chips(1 ounce), crushed (about ¾ cup)
¼ to ½ teaspoon onion powder
¼ teaspoon salt
¼ teaspoon black pepper
6 slices cheese slices

Directions

Mix all the ingredients together in a bowl, except the cheese
Form the ground beef mixture into 6 patties
Cook the patties on the grill until no longer pink in the middle
Top with cheese slices
Once the cheese is melted remove from the grill/

Best Grilled Burgers

Ingredients

1 lb lean hamburger
¼ teaspoon garlic powder
¼ teaspoon onion salt
¼ teaspoon seasoning salt
½ teaspoon Worcestershire sauce
1 egg, beaten
8 single Saltine crackers, crushed
1 slice of cheese, per burger

Directions

Mix all of the ingredients and shape into burgers
Grill to desired doneness
Top with a slice of either Provolone or Swiss cheese
Add oregano for Italian flavor, or taco seasoning for Tex-Mex flavor

Chile Con Queso Cheeseburger

Ingredients
2 Anaheim chilies
2 jalapeño peppers
Extra virgin olive oil (EVOO)
1 large garlic clove, unpeeled
1 tablespoon tomatoes, finely diced into very tiny cubes, no seeds
¼ teaspoon cumin
¼ teaspoon chili powder
½ cup Monterrey Jack cheese, shredded, Caciotta is a worthy option
½ cup cheddar cheese or ½ cup longhorn cheese, shredded
Salt & freshly ground black pepper
1 ½ lbs ground beef
4 kaiser rolls or 4 onion-topped hamburger buns, split
Lettuce leaf
Sliced onion
Sliced tomatoes
Mayonnaise and Ketchup

Directions
Light the grill, when hot, brush the grate with oil
Put the Anaheims in a small bowl with olive oil and toss
Thread jalapeños & garlic onto a metal skewer, or a wooden skewer soaked in water
Grill until blackened
Repeat with the Anaheims using grill tongs to turn
Peel and remove stems and seeds from the chilies and discard
Peel garlic
Add tomatoes to a small bowl
Chop the chile peppers and garlic and add to the tomatoes
Fold in the cheese
Sprinkle with cumin, and chili powder and season with salt and pepper, then toss
Cut eight, 6 -inch squares of wax paper
Divide the beef amongst them. Pat each portion into a 5-inch round patty
Mound one-fourth of the cheese mixture in the centers of 4 patties
Top with the remaining patties and press the edges closed
Brush with oil and season with salt and pepper
Brush the insides of the rolls with oil.
Brush the grate with more oil and grill the burgers over a hot fire
Place the burgers on lightly toasted rolls and top with lettuce leaves, onion and tomato.

Feta Burgers With Grilled Red Onions

Ingredients
3 lbs lean ground beef
1 cup feta cheese, packed, crumbled
2 teaspoons dried oregano
1 ½ teaspoons salt
1 ½ teaspoons ground black pepper
8 large garlic cloves, peeled
½ cup extra virgin olive oil
1 teaspoon extra virgin olive oil
Nonstick vegetable oil cooking spray
2 medium red onions, peeled, each cut crosswise into 4 slices
8 hamburger buns
2 large tomatoes, each one cut crosswise into 4 slices

Directions
Break up beef in large bowl
Sprinkle feta, oregano, salt, and pepper over the meat, then toss
Divide into 8 portion
Form into 4 ½ inch burgers
Press thumb into the center of the raw hamburger to make an indentation
Stuffed each burger cavity with feta cheese
Cover
Chill
Puree garlic in processor, gradually add ½ cup oil
Process for 30 seconds
Cover
Chill.
Spray grill rack with nonstick spray.
Preheat grill to medium-high
Brush the onion slices with 1 the garlic oil
Sprinkle with salt and pepper
Place burgers and onions on grill
Cover
Cook until onions are charred and burgers are medium-well, about 4 minutes longer.
Transfer to plate
Brush cut sides of buns with garlic oil and place buns, cut side down, on grill
Toast about 1 minute until heated, about 1 minute
Place burgers on bun bottoms, top each with onion, tomato, and top of the bun

Lipton Onion Burgers

Ingredients
1 1/8 ounces Lipton Recipe Secrets onion soup mix (one envelope)
2 lbs ground beef
½ cup water
1 egg
2 Tbsp hoisin sauce
½ cup breadcrumbs, dry and unseasoned

Directions
In a large mixing bowl add all of the ingredients to the ground beef
Mix until well combined
Shape into eight patties
Grill, or broil, until done
Serve with your favorite condiments

Nota bene: Also consider Beefy Onion, Onion Mushroom, Savory Herb with Garlic or Ranch Soup Mix

Jalapeño Popper Burgers

Ingredients
2 lbs ground beef
1 tablespoon Worcestershire sauce
½ teaspoon salt
½ teaspoon garlic powder
¼ teaspoon black pepper
4 ounces cream cheese, softened
½ teaspoon dried ancho chile powder
½ teaspoon ground cumin
1 tablespoon dried onion flakes
1 to 2 tablespoon minced jalapeño pepper, seeded, to taste

Directions
Mix the meat, with Worcestershire sauce, salt, garlic powder, and pepper
Shape the mixture into 12 thin patties, each one about 4 inches in diameter
Mix the cream cheese, ancho chili powder, cumin, dried onion, and minced jalapeño
Top 6 patties with the cheese mixture, spreading to within ½. inch of the edge
Cover each patty with one of the remaining 6 patties, sealing the edges well
Broil, or grill, (4 inches from the heat), until preferred doneness and cheese is melted
Top with a bit of grated cheddar, and guacamole

Nota bene: If the mixture is stiff and difficult to spread, warm it in the microwave for about 15 seconds.

Cream Cheese Stuffed Garlic Burgers

Ingredients

2 lbs hamburger meat
10 Tblsp instant minced garlic
½ teaspoon salt
¼ teaspoon ground pepper
6 ounces cream cheese with garlic and herbs

Directions

Put hamburger meat in a bowl and add garlic, salt and pepper
Mix together until just blended
Make 12 patties no more than 1-inch thick
Spread cream cheese in the center of 6 patties, approximately 1 oz. per patty.
Don't spread all the way to the edge
Put remaining patties on top of the cream cheese and seal along the circumference
Grill on high to your desired taste. (About 8-10 minutes)

Nota bene: Be advised it takes longer than normal for these burgers to cook because of the cream cheese.

Buffalo Sauce Burgers Stuffed
With Blue Cheese

Ingredients

4 Tblsp butter, cut in small pieces
1⁄3 cup mild hot sauce (Durkee, Frank's RedHot)
½ cup finely crumbled Blue cheese
1 tablespoon minced garlic
2 lbs 85% lean ground beef , or 2 lbs ground buffalo meat
½ teaspoon celery seed
1⁄3 cup finely chopped onion
6 hamburger buns, split

Directions

Melt butter and whisk in hot sauce
Mix blue cheese and garlic in a small bowl
Gently mix beef (or buffalo), celery seed, onion and ¼ cup hot sauce
Form into 12 patties, about 4 ½ inches in diameter and no more than ½ inch thick
Spoon about 2 teaspoons of cheese-garlic mixture into the center of 6 patties
Top with remaining patties and press
Seal the edges to keep the Blue cheese from oozing out
Cover and refrigerate until ready to grill
Heat the BBQ grill to medium heat and oil its grate
Grill the burgers about 4 to 5 minutes on each side, or until cooked to taste
Brush with remaining hot sauce mixture during last 2 minutes of cooking
Toast the buns

Nota bene: Buffalo sauce is a mixture of melted butter and hot sauce typically served on fried chicken wings (Buffalo wings).

Gordon Ramsay's Ultimate Burger

Ingredients

1 lb ground sirloin
1 onion, minced
1 tablespoon ketchup
1 tablespoon sun-dried tomato, cut thinly
¼ cup garlic, chopped
½ teaspoon Worcestershire sauce
½ teaspoon Tabasco sauce
½ teaspoon honey mustard

Directions

Combine all ingredients
Form into patties
Cook as desired

Canadian Burger
With Beer-Braised Onions and Cheddar

Ingredients
1 tablespoon butter
1 large onion, thinly sliced
1 tablespoon sugar
3/4 cup beer
1 ½ lbs fresh ground beef or 1 ½ lbs ground round
2 garlic cloves, minced
¼ cup finely diced red pepper
¼ cup beer
2 Tblsp Dijon mustard
Salt & freshly ground black pepper
2 cups grated cheddar cheese

Directions
Melt the butter in a large heavy skillet
Add the onions
Cook, stirring frequently over medium heat for 5 to 6 minutes, or until tender.
Add ¾ cup beer and the sugar
Cook until beer is absorbed and the onions become lightly browned, about 15 minutes

Pre-heat the barbecue to high
Gently combine beef, garlic, red pepper, ¼ cup beer, Dijon, salt & pepper
Form into 4 patties 1-inch thick, and place on the grill, turning heat down to medium
Grill for 4 to 6 minutes per side, until nearly done.
Top each burger with ½ cup grated cheese
Heat until slightly melted
Serve on toasted buns
Top with the beer-braised onions

Korean Hamburgers

Ingredients
1 lb ground beef
4 Tblsp soy sauce
2 Tblsp sugar
1 tablespoon sesame seeds
1 tablespoon vegetable oil
3 Tblsp chopped green onions
1 tablespoon minced garlic
1 dash black pepper

Directions
Mix all of ingredients thoroughly
Shape into 4 patties
Grill, or fry
Serve on a bun with teriyaki sauce

Floozy Burger

Ingredients

1⁄3 cup sweet onions or 1⁄3 cup Vidalia onion, is best
1⁄3 cup dill pickle
½-1 cup mayonnaise
2 cups finely chopped lettuce
2 lbs ground beef
2 teaspoons Cajun seasoning
1 teaspoon pepper
8 slices tomatoes
8 ounces sliced mushrooms, sauteed in butter
8 slices cheese
8 fried eggs (One per burger)
4 or 8 hamburger buns (a topless floozy only needs 4)

Directions

Mix sweet onion, dill pickle, mayonnaise and finely chopped lettuce
Set aside
Fry eggs until no longer runny
Set aside
Mix ground beef, Cajun seasoning and pepper
Form into 8 burgers
Fry burgers until they are no longer pink inside
Set aside and top with a slice of tomato
Saute mushrooms in butter and portion out onto burgers Immediately
Top with cheese and Fried Egg
Top with the slaw condiments
No bun on top

Nota bene: This is a **topless,** open-faced burger. You know, a floozy

Mushroom Swiss Burger

Ingredients
1 teaspoon extra virgin olive oil
2 ounces mushrooms, finely chopped
1 small garlic clove, sliced
1/8 teaspoon kosher salt
4 ounces 90% lean ground sirloin
1 scallion, finely chopped
1 tablespoon soy sauce
¼ teaspoon fresh ground black pepper
1 slice Swiss cheese (½ ounce)
1 seeded hamburger bun, toasted
1 tablespoon Dijon mustard
2 small romaine lettuce leaves
2 slices tomatoes (¼ inch thick)

Directions
Preheat broiler with oven rack about 6 inches from direct heat source
Preheat oil in a small skillet set over medium heat.
Add mushrooms, garlic and salt
Cook until mushrooms have released their liquid and turned golden brown, 5 minutes.
Set aside
Cool
In a medium bowl combine sirloin, scallion, soy sauce, pepper and cooled mushrooms
Mix lightly
Form into a patty
Place on a broiler pan.
Broil until cooked, about 3 minutes per side for medium.
Top with Swiss cheese while piping hot.
Spread each side of the bun with mustard
Top with lettuce, tomato and the burger.

Taco Burgers
With Chipotle Mayo

Ingredients
1 lb lean ground beef
½ cup of your favorite salsa
1 large egg
0. 5 (1 ¼ ounce) package taco seasoning mix
1/3 cup mayonnaise
1 Chipotle chile pepper in adobo (from a 4 oz. can of Chipotle peppers in adobo sauce)
Chopped jalapeños (optional)
Sliced tomatoes
Chopped fresh cilantro
Chopped red onion
Monterey jack pepper cheese

Directions
Combine the beef, ½ cup salsa, egg and the ½ packet of taco seasoning
Mix in a large bowl
Shape into 4 even burgers.
Place the mayonnaise and Chipotle chile in the blender
Cover and blend to a smooth consistency
Grill or broil burgers, turning once, until desired doneness.
Towards the end of cooking , place a slice of Monterey jack pepper cheese on patty
Serve on buns
Top with Chipotle, chile mayonnaise, sliced tomatoes, cilantro and red onion
Serve with corn tortilla chips on the side

Doctor Louie's Hamburger Patties

Ingredients
2 lbs lean ground beef
2 large eggs, beaten
½ cup finely chopped onion
½ cup crushed soda crackers, or ½ cup fine dry breadcrumb
3/4 teaspoon granulated garlic powder
½ teaspoon salt
½ teaspoon black pepper
4 Tblsp hickory barbecue sauce
6 Tblsp olive oil (for frying)

Directions
Combine beef, eggs, onions, crackers, garlic powder, salt, pepper and barbecue sauce
Mix until well incorporated
Portion the hamburger patties to weigh 6 to 7 ounces each
Press together and flatten to a thickness of about 3 ½ inches in diameter
Press an indentation in the center of the hamburger patty
In a frying pan over medium-high heat, heat olive oil
Place 3 patties in the hot oil and fry for 2 to 3 minutes
As the burger cooks, notice how the indentation in the patty begins to close
Turn the patty over and continue to fry for another 2 to 3 minutes
Serve on warmed, buttered bun.
Top with mayonnaise, Dijon mustard, slices of sweet onion and tomato, lettuce

Nota bene: Other appropriate topping options include a slice of Swiss cheese, a pickle, fried mushrooms and fried, caramelized onions spread over the top of the entrée.

Brew Burger

Ingredients

1 ½ lbs ground beef
1 large Vidalia onion, cut in slices
4 slices Swiss cheese
4 slices tomatoes
Lettuce
4 hamburger buns
¼ cup Heinz 57 steak sauce
¼ cup beer

Directions

Combine sauce ingredients
Microwave on high (in a glass measuring cup) for 1 to 1 ½ minutes, until bubbly
Set aside
Shape ground beef into patties (approx. ¾" thick)
Place onion slices on grill over medium coals
Grill onions, uncovered, for about 4 minutes
Add patties
Grill onions and burgers uncovered for 13 to 15 minutes, turning occasionally
Season burgers with salt
Just before before the burgers are done, brush with sauce.
Remember to reserve some sauce for topping.
Top with cheese.
Remove from grill.
Place on buns and top burgers with reserved sauce

Texas Squealer Burger

Ingredients

1 ½ lbs 80% lean ground beef

12 slices bacon, uncooked

1. 1 ½tablespoon grill seasoning (McCormicks Mesquite)

1 teaspoon garlic powder

1 tablespoon minced dried onion

¼ cup Worcestershire sauce

Salt and pepper

Directions

Slice the bacon in half, then in strips, then dice

Gently mix all ingredients in a large bowl

Add the bacon.

Form into 6 to 8 patties

Grill patties approximately 5 minutes on each side

Rest the burgers for 5 minutes before serving

Top with cheese and favorite condiments

Nota bene: Resist the urge to food process the bacon because doing so would make it gummy.

Cowboy Burgers

Ingredients
2 Tblsp olive oil
3 onions, thinly sliced, separated into rings
8 hamburger patties (¼ lb. each)
3 Tblsp A-1 Original Sauce
2 tomatoes, sliced
8 hamburger buns, partially split
8 slices Cheddar cheese

Directions
Preheat grill to medium heat
Heat oil in large nonstick skillet to medium-high heat
Add onions
Cook 5 minutes, stirring frequently
Cover with lid
Simmer 20 minutes, or until onions are golden brown
Stir frequently
Grill patties 5 minute on each side or until medium doneness (160ºF)
Stir steak sauce into onion mixture
Place 1 tomato slice and burger on bottom half of each bun
Cover with 1 slice cheese, 3 Tblsp of the onion mixture and the top of bun

Southwest Burger

Ingredients
1 lb ground buffalo meat
2 teaspoons taco seasoning
1/3 cup salsa
¼ cup guacamole
¼ cup sour cream
3 slices jalapeño jack cheese
canned green chili
lettuce, shredded
1 tomato, diced
French fried onion rings
3 buns

Directions
Mix together bison burger meat, taco seasoning and salsa
Shape into 3 burgers
Grill on medium heat on foil for 6 to 8 minutes each side
Mix together sour cream and guacamole
Top the burgers with cheese
Grill an additional 2 minutes to melt the cheese
Place burger on bun
Top with green chilies, diced tomatoes, french fried onions and shredded lettuce
Spread sour cream/guacamole mixture on top of bun and place on top of burger

Nota bene: Grilling the bison burger on top of foil holds the burger together.

Blu Moon Burgers

Ingredients
1 lb ground beef
4 large toasted hamburger buns
4 ounces crumbled blue cheese
4 ounces softened cream cheese
4 slices Monterey jack cheese
Condiments
Mayonnaise
Shaved onion (Bermuda)
Lettuce
Tomatoes

Directions
Combine blue cheese and cream cheese and beat together well
Set aside in order to give the flavors time to meld together
Form the ground beef into 4 patties
Salt and pepper
Cook to taste
When done, add ¼ of the blue cheese mixture to the top of each burger
Top with a slice of jack cheese
Spread mayo on toasted buns
Once the Jack cheese begins to go gooey, place the burgers on buns
Add remaining condiments

Nota bene: Ketchup and blue cheese flavors clash, so don't dress with ketchup.

Almost White Castle/ Krystal Sliders

Ingredients
1 ½ lbs ground chuck
1 envelope (4 tablespoons) onion soup mix
1 egg
½ teaspoon pepper
2 Tblsp water
1/3 cup breadcrumbs
24 small square dinner rolls
American cheese (optional)
Pickle, optional
½ cup mustard
½ cup ketchup

Directions
Preheat oven to 400°F
Mix first 6 ingredients and press into an ungreased 10- by 15-inch pan
Prick with a fork
Bake for 10 minutes
Drain off juices
Cool
Cut into 24 squares
Place squares on dinner rolls
Combine mustard and ketchup and spread onto the rolls
Top with pickles and cheese

Nota bene: To freeze:
Assemble hamburgers minus any condiments.
Wrap in plastic wrap.
Store in a Ziploc bag and label.
Freeze.

To reheat: Microwave until heated clear through.
Add condiments.

Perfect Burger

Ingredients

1 ½ pounds ground chuck (80 percent lean
Kosher salt and freshly ground black pepper
1 ½ Tblsp canola oil
4 slices cheese (optional)
4 hamburger buns, split; toasted, if desired

Directions

Divide the meat into 4 equal portions (about 6 ounces each)
Form each portion loosely into a ¾-inch-thick burger
Season both sides of each burger with salt and pepper
Heat a gas grill to high, or charcoal grill until the coals glow bright orange and ash over
Brush the burgers with the oil.
Flip over the burgers.
Cook beef burgers until golden brown and slightly charred on the flip side

Or, on a griddle or cast iron pan, heat the oil over high heat until it begins to shimmer
Cook the burgers until golden brown and slightly charred on the first side (3 to 5 min)
Flip over the burgers.
Cook the beef burgers until golden brown

Bacon and Kimchi Burgers

Ingredients

¼ cup sambal oelek (Indonesian chile sauce)
¼ cup mayonnaise
¼ cup ketchup
4 slices of thick-cut bacon
11 ¼ pounds ground beef chuck
Kosher salt
4 slices of American cheese
4 potato buns, toasted
1 cup chopped drained cabbage kimchi (6 ounces)

Directions

In a small bowl, combine sambal with the mayonnaise and ketchup and mix well
Light a grill or preheat a cast iron fry pan
Grill the bacon over moderate heat, turning, until golden and crisp, about 5 minutes
Drain the greasy bacon on paper towels
Form the beef into eight, ¼-inch-thick burgers and season with salt
Grill over high heat, turning, until browned, 1 minute per side
Make 4 stacks of 2 burgers each on the grill and spoon 1 tablespoon of the sambal mayo over each stack.
Top with the cheese
Cover and grill over high heat until the cheese is melted, about 1 minute
Spread the remaining sambal mayo on the bottom buns
Top with the burgers, bacon and kimchi, close and serve.

The Ultimate Burger

Ingredients:
1 lb. lean ground beef
1 cup All-Bran Buds cereal
1 large egg, lightly beaten
¼ cup onion, finely chopped
2 Tblsp BBQ sauce
1 tsp. Worcestershire sauce
½ tsp. each, salt and fresh cracked pepper
½ cup cup Cheddar cheese, grated
1 tsp. vegetable oil

Directions
Combine all of the many ingredients
Mix until just combined and shape into 4 patties
Avoid over mixing to ensure burgers will not be tough
In a large cast iron skillet, heat oil over medium-high heat
Cook patties for 4 minutes per side, or until cooked through
Alternatively, cook on a greased grill over medium-high heat for 3 minutes per side.
Serve on a toasted bun with your favorite condiments.

Chipotle Burger
With Caramelized Red Onions

Ingredients:

2 Tblsp olive oil
1 large red onion, halved, thinly sliced
2 Tblsp balsamic vinegar
2-½ pounds lean ground beef
4 Chipotle peppers with adobo sauce from a can,
¼ cup minced fresh cilantro
1 garlic clove, minced
1 tablespoon grated lime zest
Generous pinch of salt
A few grinds black pepper
8 slices Monterey Jack cheese
8 whole grain hamburger buns, toasted
Mayonnaise or other condiments as desired

Directions

Heat oil in a large skillet over medium heat.
Add onion and cook, stirring often, for 15 minutes or until the onions are golden brown
Drizzle with vinegar and stir to combine
Remove from heat and keep warm
Preheat grill. medium-high heat
In a large bowl, combine beef, Chipotle, cilantro, garlic, lime zest, salt and pepper
Mix well
Form beef into eight patties
Oil the grill grate and grill burgers for five minutes
Flip and grill for another four minutes
Lay slices of cheese over burgers
Cook for another one to two minutes or until burgers are cooked through.
Slather the buns with mayonnaise and/or other condiments.
Place burgers on the bottoms of the buns.
Top with caramelized onions.

Blue-Cheese Stuffed Burgers on Ciabatta Rolls

Ingredients:
2-½ pounds lean ground beef
½ teaspoon salt
Freshly ground black pepper. taste
1 cup crumbled blue cheese, crumbled feta, divided.
8 Ciabatta rolls, split, toasted
Honey mustard dressing
Tomato slices
Spinach leaves

Directions:
Preheat grill to a medium-high temperature
In a large bowl combine ground beef, salt and pepper
Divide the beef into eight portions
Flatten each portion into a thick patty
Press an indentation in the top of each with your thumb
Place two Tblsp of blue cheese into each indentation
Use hands to close the patty around the cheese, sealing it in, to make a ball
Press each ball into a patty
Grease the grill grate
Grill the burgers for five to six minutes per side, or until cooked through
Spread or brush Ciabatta rolls with honey mustard dressing
Place burgers on the bottom halves of the rolls
Top with tomato slices and spinach leaves

Tokyo Burger

Ingredients

1 pound mixed ground pork and ground beef
1 Tblsp Mustard
1 Egg
2 Tbsp butter
4 slices Cheese
1 ripe Avocado, sliced into wedges
2 Beetroot cooked
Cress
5 Bread rolls

Directions

Heat the grill
Slice the tops off of all five bread rolls and cut each one in half
Soften the fifth bread roll in lukewarm water, then squeeze the water out
Mix the pork and beef mince with the mustard, salt and pepper, egg and softened roll
Form the mixture into 4 hamburgers
Heat the butter in a pan and fry the hamburgers until brown, turning several times
Place a slice of cheese on each burger and put under the hot grill
Melt the cheese
Toast the bread roll halves quickly under the grill
Place one cheeseburger on each half roll and top with a few avocado wedges
Garnish with beetroot strips and cress
Serve at once.

Burger With Blue Cheese and Fried Onions

Ingredients

1 lb. Ground Beef
1 Red chili pepper, de-seeded and finely chopped
2 Cloves garlic
1 Egg, beaten
4 Tblsp Olive oil
4 Onions
4 Tblsp Mayonnaise
5 – 6 ounces Blue Cheese, crumbled
4 Watercress, 4 sprigs
1 Tbsp Ketchup
4 Buns

Directions

Mix the ground beef with the chopped chili and garlic
Season with salt and pepper
Mix in the beaten egg.
Form into 4 burgers and set aside
Heat the oil in a deep frying pan
Slowly fry the onions until browned, stirring frequently to avoid burning
Mix the mayonnaise with the ketchup
Toast the burger buns
When the onions are cooked, remove them from the pan
Wipe the pan clean and add a little more oil
Fry the burgers for 3 minutes on each side or until cooked through
Place a dollop of onions on the bottom of the bun
Add the burger, cheese, watercress and mayonnaise and serve immediately

Spicy Peanut Butter Bacon Sliders

Ingredients
2 pounds ground beef
¼ cup soy sauce
2 Tblsps Sriracha
½ cup creamy peanut butter, divided
1 pinch pepper
6 Tblsps butter, softened
12 whole slider buns
12 slices pepper jack or cheddar cheese
12 slices cooked bacon
2 whole jalapeños, sliced
2 cups crispy French fries
1 whole purple onion, sliced

Directions
Preheat a grill to medium-high heat
Mix ground beef, soy sauce, Sriracha, 2 Tblsps of the peanut butter, a pinch of pepper
Divide the beef in 12 balls and flatten each into a patty the size of the slider buns.
Butter both halves of each bun
When the grill is medium high, place the patties on the grill and cook for 4 minutes
Flip the patties over with a spatula and cook to desired doneness.
During the last 2 minutes of cooking, place a slice of cheese on the top of each patty
Close the grill lid to melt the cheese
Remove the sliders to a plate and cover with foil
Place buttered slider buns cut side down on the grill for 1-2 minutes
Toast them
Divide the remaining peanut butter among the 12 bottom buns
Top each with a burger patty, a slice of bacon, jalapeños, crispy fries and red onion
Drizzle with Sriracha
Cover with the top of the bun and serve

Pimento Cheese Sliders

Ingredients:
16 slices white or wheat bread
1 ½ lbs ground beef sirloin
2 to 3 garlic cloves, grated or finely chopped
3 to 4 Tbsp gated onion
1 Tbsp paprika or sweet smoked paprika
½ cup lager beer
Salt and pepper
Olive Oil
2 Tbsp butter
2 Tbsp flour
1 cup milk
1 cup shredded sharp yellow cheddar cheese
3 Tbsp well-drained chopped pimentos
1 Tbsp yellow mustard
Several drops of hot sauce
8 slices dill pickle chips

Directions:
Heat the oven. 350 degrees F.
With a biscuit cutter, cut the bread into 3-inch rounds, or trim into slider sized squares
Arrange on a baking sheet and bake until lightly toasted and golden, 8 to 10 minutes
Combine the meat with the garlic, onion, paprika, beer, salt and pepper
Mix and form 8 burger about 3 inches in diameter
Drizzle with olive oil
Heat a griddle pan or large cast-iron skillet over medium-high heat
Cook the patties for 3 to 4 minutes per side
Melt the butter over medium heat
Whisk in the flour and milk and simmer
Allow to thicken for about 3 minutes
Season with salt and pepper
Melt in the cheese and stir in the pimentos, mustard and hot sauce
Divide the patties among 8 toast slices
Top with the cheese sauce and another slice of toast
Garnish with pickles secured with toothpicks

Gingery Steak and Brie Sliders With Balsamic Cranberry Sauce

Ingredients

5 pounds bone-in short ribs
2 Tblsps olive oil
Salt and pepper
¼ cup soy sauce
¼ cup Worcestershire sauce
½ cup balsamic vinegar
½ cup red wine (or chicken broth)
4 cloves garlic, minced or grated
1 tablespoon fresh ginger, grated
8 ounces Brie, sliced
Arugula, for topping
20 to 30 sliders buns, toasted
Balsamic Cranberry Sauce
1 ½ cup fresh cranberries
1/3 cup balsamic vinegar
1/3 cup water
¼ cup brown sugar
1 teaspoon fresh rosemary, chopped
2 teaspoons fresh ginger, grated

Directions

The night before, heat a large heavy bottom skillet over medium high-heat. Add the olive oil and ribs to the skillet and sprinkle with salt & pepper Sear the ribs on all sides, about 1 minute per side. Remove the ribs and place them in crockpot or dutch oven. Add the ribs, soy sauce, Worcestershire sauce, balsamic vinegar, red wine, garlic and ginger to the bowl of a crockpot. Add1 to 3 cups of water until the ribs are half way submerged. Cover and slow cook 6-8 hours or on high for 4-6 hours or until the meat shreds easily. Shred the meat and keep on the warm setting until serving time.

Add the ribs, soy sauce, Worcestershire sauce, balsamic vinegar, red wine, garlic and ginger to a cast iron dutch oven or oven safe pot with a tight fighting lid. Add water until the ribs are at least half way submerged, there should be about 1 to 2 cups. Cover and cook in a preheated the oven to 325 degrees F. for 2 ½ to 3 hours or until the meat shreds easily. Shred the meat and keep covered on low heat (about 200-250 degrees F) until serving time. (Balsamic Cranberry Sauce). Add the cranberries, balsamic vinegar, water, brown sugar, rosemary and ginger to medium size pot and place over medium-high heat. Bring to a boil and then reduce the heat to a simmer. Simmer for 5-10 minutes or until the sauce has thickened. Season with salt and pepper. Add the shredded warm meat to the bottom of a slider bun. Top with sliced brie. The brie should melt over the warm meat, but if not, place under the broiler for 30 seconds. Top with cranberry sauce and arugula. Sandwich with the top bun.

Summer Strawberry Sliders
With Blue Cheese Sauce

Ingredients:
(for the blue cheese sauce)
¼ cup mayonnaise
¼ cup sour cream
1 tablespoon white vinegar
4 teaspoons granulated sugar
Salt & pepper,. taste
2 oz. blue cheese, crumbled

(for the burgers)
1 lb. ground beef
Salt & pepper
1 cup sliced strawberries
¼ cup chopped sweet onions
Lettuce
16 slider rolls or sandwich bread cut out into circles

Directions:
Preheat outdoor grill to medium high heat
In a small bowl, stir together all ingredients for the blue cheese sauce
Refrigerate
Divide the ground beef into 16 even portions
Form into mini burger patties the size of the slider rolls
Sprinkle with salt and pepper
Grill about 1-2 minutes per side, or until cooked thoroughly
Rest for 5 minutes, then assemble the sliders
To assemble, place lettuce on the bottom of the slider roll
Top with burger, strawberry slices, diced onion and blue cheese sauce
Top with other half of roll
Serve immediately

Slow Cooker
Mini Meatball Sliders

Ingredients
1 egg, beaten
1/3 cup bread crumbs
¼ cup whole milk
¼ cup Parmigiano Reggiano, grated
¼ cup onion, minced
1 clove garlic, minced
4 pounds ground beef
2 cups of spaghetti sauce
Slider rolls

What. Do:
Combine the egg, bread crumbs, milk, Parmigiano Reggiano cheese, onion and garlic
Add ground beef to the bread crumb mixture and mix well
Use a big spoon to scoop out 24 meatballs (1.5- to 2-ounces each)
Shape into balls with your hands
Place inside a slow cooker liner inside the slow cooker bowl.
Fit the liner snugly against the bottom and sides of the bowl
Pull top of liner over rim of bowl.
Place meatballs into liner, then turn slow cooker to 275 degrees
Place lid on slow cooker
Cook for approximately 1 hour or until meatballs are thoroughly cooked
Add sauce and continue cooking an additional 10 to 15 minutes until sauce is warm
Carefully remove lid to allow steam to escape
P;ace a meatball on a slider bun and drizzle of sauce onto it
Afterwards, let the slow cooker cool completely before removing liner

Nota bene: Instead of spraying the inside of the slow cooker with non-stick cooking spray, which requires washing afterwards, use Reynolds Slow Cooker Liners (No washing required.)

Aussie Burgers W/Pickled Beets, Pineapple and Fried Eggs

Ingredients
1 red beet (8 ounces), scrubbed
2 teaspoons extra-virgin olive oil
Kosher salt
1 small white onion, thinly sliced
1 ¼ cups distilled white vinegar
½ cup rice vinegar
2 tablespoons sugar
Four ¼-inch-thick slices of fresh pineapple
Crushed red pepper
2 ½ tablespoons unsalted butter
4 large eggs

Directions
Preheat the oven. 350°
In a small bowl, coat the beet with 1 teaspoon of EVOO,
Sprinkle with a generous pinch of salt
Wrap the beet in foil and roast on a pie plate until tender, 1 hour
Let cool, then peel the beet and slice it ¼ inch thick
Transfer to a heatproof bowl and add the onion
Combine the white vinegar, rice vinegar, sugar & 2 ½ tablespoons of salt in a saucepan
Bring to a boil
Reduce to moderate heat
Add sugar, stir to dissolve the sugar
Pour the brine over the beet and onion
Let it cool, about 1 hour
Light a grill or preheat a grill pan.
Coat pineapple slices with 1 tsp of olive oil a pinch each of salt and crushed red pepper
Grill the pineapple until warm and lightly charred, 2 minutes per side.
Transfer to a plate and keep warm
In a large nonstick skillet, melt the butter
Add the eggs
Cook over moderate heat until the whites set and yolks are slightly runny, 3 minutes
Remove from the heat and season with salt.
Layer the pickled beets and onions
Top with the grilled pineapple rings and the fried eggs

Nota bene: Pickled beets can be refrigerated for up to 2 weeks.

Cheddar-Stuffed Burgers With Pickled Slaw and Fried Shallots

Ingredients
Kosher salt
8 cups finely shredded green cabbage (1 ½ pound head)
1 cup distilled white vinegar
1 tablespoon sugar
2 tablespoons yellow mustard seeds
Vegetable oil, for frying
5 large shallots, sliced very thinly crosswise and separated into rings
¼ cup Wondra flour
1 ½ pounds ground rib eye steak and pork fatback
1 teaspoon onion powder
1 teaspoon garlic powder
1 teaspoon sweet smoked paprika
1 tablespoon Worcestershire sauce
Freshly ground pepper
6 ounces extra-sharp cheddar, shredded
2 cups baby arugula
4 Brioche buns, split and toasted

Directions
In a large bowl, toss one tablespoon of kosher salt with the cabbage. Massage the cabbage until the leaves softens and release their liquid, about 4 minutes. Drain the cabbage in a colander and rinse. Wipe out the bowl. Add the vinegar, sugar, mustard seeds, 1 cup of water and 1 tablespoon of salt. Add the cabbage to the vinegar mixture. Toss, coat and place a plate on top to keep it submerged. Let stand at room temperature for two hours. In a large saucepan, heat 1 ½ inches of vegetable oil to 325°. In a medium bowl, toss the shallots with the Wondra flour, Fry the shallots all at once, stirring gently, until golden, about 7 minutes . Use a slotted spoon. Transfer the shallots to a paper towel–lined plate. Drain. Season the shallots with salt. Reserve the cooking oil. Combine the ground beef with the onion powder, garlic powder, smoked paprika, Worcestershire sauce and 2 teaspoons each of kosher salt and ground pepper. Knead gently until thoroughly mixed. Form the beef into eight, 4-inch patties. Press the shredded cheese into four 2 ½. inch disks. Sandwich the cheese disks between the patties Pinch around the periphery of the patties to seal. Heat a grill pan or griddle. Brush the burgers with some shallot cooking oil. Cook over moderate heat until browned on the bottom, about 3 minutes. Flip the burgers. Invert a large heatproof bowl over them. Cook until medium within and the cheese is melted, about 3 minutes longer the arugula on the bun bottoms and top with the burgers . Drain the pickled cabbage. Mound cabbage on the burgers. Reserve the rest of the pickled cabbage for another time
Top with the fried shallots and the bun top s and serve

Bacon Burgers On Brioche Buns

Ingredients
2 medium red onions, thinly sliced
6 tablespoons extra-virgin olive oil, plus more for brushing
½ cup mayonnaise
2 tablespoons of fresh lemon juice
Salt and freshly ground pepper
8 slices of thick-cut bacon (12 ounces)
3 pounds mixed ground chuck and ground sirloin
12 ounces of Brie, sliced
8 Brioche burger buns, split

Directions
Preheat the oven to 400°
On a rimmed baking sheet, toss the onions with 2 tablespoons of the olive oil
Roast until softened, about 20 minutes
Whisk the mayonnaise with the lemon juice
Gradually whisk in the remaining ¼ cup of olive oil and season with salt and pepper
Cook the bacon In a large skillet over moderately high heat, until crisp
Drain on paper towels and break each strip in half
Light a grill or preheat a grill pan
Form the ground meat into eight patties
Season generously with salt and pepper and brush with olive oil
Grill over moderately high heat until well-browned on the bottom, 5 minutes
Flip the burgers
Mound the Brie on top
Grill for 4 minutes longer, until cheese is slightly melted and burgers are medium-rare
Spread the lemon mayonnaise on the cut sides of the buns
Set the burgers on the bottoms and top with the bacon and onions
Close the burgers and serve right away

Umami Burgers
With Port and Stilton

Ingredients
1 cup Ruby port
2 pounds mixed ground beef brisket, skirt steak and sirloin steak (20 percent fat)
Salt and freshly ground pepper
½ cup Stilton cheese (3 ounces), softened
Umami dust for sprinkling (optional)
4 Brioche hamburger buns, buttered and toasted

Directions
Cook the port wine over moderate heat until reduced to 2 Tbsp, about 15 minutes
Heat a cast-iron griddle until very hot
Form meat into four, 4-inch in diameter by-1-inch thick patties without packing tightly
Season generously with salt and pepper
Arrange the patties on the griddle
Cover with a roasting pan
Cook over moderately high heat for 4 minutes, until very crusty.
Flip the patties and cook, covered, for 2 minutes longer;
Top with the Stilton
Cook uncovered for 1 minute
Transfer the patties. a plate and sprinkle with the umami dust
Rest for 2 minutes and set on the buns
Drizzle with the reduced port, top with the buns and serve

Nota bene: To make simplified umami dust, use a spice grinder to pulse 3 tablespoons of bonito flakes, ½ ounce crumbled dried kombu and ½ ounce dried shitake mushrooms into a powder.

.

Pug Burger

Ingredients
2 pounds lean, ground sirloin
8 strips applewood-smoked bacon
½ cup mayonnaise, plus more for serving
1 garlic clove, minced
Kosher salt and freshly ground pepper
4 kaiser rolls, split
3 tablespoons extra-virgin olive oil
3 ounces Danish blue cheese, sliced
Sliced, ripe, Hass avocado
Bibb lettuce leaves
Red onion slices

Directions
Light the grill.
Form the meat into 4 large patties about 1 inch thick
Let stand at room temperature for 30 minutes
In a skillet, cook the bacon over moderate heat until crisp, 6 minutes
Drain the grease off the bacon on paper towels.
In a bowl, mix the ½ cup of mayonnaise with the garlic
Season with salt and pepper
Brush the cut sides of the rolls with 2 tablespoons of the oil and lightly toast on the grill
Brush the burgers with the remaining oil and season well with salt and pepper
Grill over moderately high heat for 3 minutes
Flip the burger and top with the cheese.
Cook for 3 more minutes, for medium-rare
Spread the bottom roll halves with the garlic mayonnaise
Top with a burger, bacon, avocado, lettuce and onion and serve

Green-Chile Burgers with Fried Eggs

Ingredients
2 ¼ pounds ground chuck
Salt and freshly ground pepper
½ pound mild American blue cheese cut into 4 thin slices
4 large eggs
4 Brioche buns, split
4 tablespoons unsalted butter, melted
Vegetable oil
1 cup Green-Chile Relish, warmed

Directions
Light the grill.
Gently form the beef into 4 thick patties
Season with salt and pepper
Grill over moderately high heat until lightly charred on outside and medium-rare inside
Just before the burgers are done, top each one with a slice of cheese and let it melt
Heat a large cast-iron skillet and brush it lightly with oil
Crack the eggs into the skillet
Cook sunny-side up over moderate heat, about 4 minutes.
Spread the cut sides of the buns with the melted butter and toast on the grill
Transfer the burgers. the buns
Top with the Green-Top with the Green-Chile Relish and the fried eggs and serve

Minetta Burger

Ingredients
2 tablespoons unsalted butter
1 large yellow onion, halved and thinly sliced
¼ cup water
Kosher salt and freshly ground pepper
2 pounds ground sirloin or a blend of beef short rib and brisket
1 tablespoon vegetable oil
5 ounces sharp cheddar cheese, thinly sliced
4 Brioche buns, split and toasted
Lettuce, tomato slices and pickles, for serving

Directions
In a large skillet, melt the butter
Add the onion
Cook over moderate heat, stirring occasionally, until deep golden, about 40 minutes
Add the water and scrape up any browned bits from the bottom of the pan
Cook until the liquid evaporates, about 5 minutes
Season the caramelized onion with salt and pepper
Keep warm
Gently shape the ground sirloin into four 1-inch-thick patties
Season generously with salt and pepper
Heat the oil in a large cast-iron skillet
Place the burgers in the skillet warmed to medium high heat.
Cook until deep brown outside and medium-rare within, about 6 minutes per side.
During the last 2 minutes, top the burgers with cheese and cover with foil to melt
Transfer the burgers to the buns
Top with the caramelized onion
Serve with lettuce, tomato and pickles.

Nota bene: Minetta Tavern Restaurant, located in the heart of Greenwich Village, is renowned for its delicious burgers, including an 8 ounce blend of prime dry-aged beef, cooked , then dressed with caramelized onions and served on a custom brioche bun.

Cheddar and Onion Smashed Burgers

Ingredients

16 thin bread-and-butter pickle slices, patted dry
Four 4-inch potato buns, buttered and toasted
1 ¼ pounds ground beef chuck
Salt and freshly ground pepper
2 small onions, sliced paper thin
4 ounces sharp cheddar cheese, sliced
Umami dust, sprinkling , optional

Directions

Heat a cast-iron griddle until very hot
Without overworking the meat, loosely form it into 4 balls and place on the griddle
Cook the meatballs over moderately high heat for 30 seconds
Using a sturdy, goodly-sized spatula, flatten each ball into a 5-inch diameter patty
Season the patties with salt and pepper
Cook for 2 minutes, until well seared
Press a handful of thinly sliced onions onto each patty
Carefully use the spatula to flip each burger so the onions are on the bottom
Top with the cheese and cook for 2 minutes
Cover with and cook just until the cheese is melted, 1 minute more
Layer the pickle slices on the bottom buns
Transfer the burgers with the onions to the buns
Sprinkle over the top of them with umami dust
Top with the buns and serve.

Cheddar BLT Burgers With Tarragon Russian Dressing

Ingredients

½ cup mayonnaise
1/3 cup ketchup
1 tablespoon red wine vinegar
1 tablespoon grated onion
1 tablespoon chopped parsley
1 tablespoon chopped tarragon
1 teaspoon Worcestershire sauce
12 ounces thickly sliced bacon
1 1/3 pounds ground beef chuck
1 1/3 pounds ground beef sirloin
1 teaspoon kosher salt
½ teaspoon freshly ground pepper
2 tablespoons unsalted butter, melted
3 ounces sharp cheddar cheese, cut into 6 slices
6 hamburger buns, split and toasted
6 iceberg lettuce leaves
6 slices of tomato
6 slices of red onion

Directions

Whisk mayo ketchup, red wine vinegar, onion, parsley, tarragon & Worcestershire sauce
Cover and refrigerate
Cook the bacon over moderately high heat, turning once, until crisp, about six minutes
Drain on a paper towel and cut the bacon into large pieces
Light the grill
Fill a large bowl with ice water
Gently mix the ground chuck with the ground sirloin, salt and pepper
Form the meat into six 4-inch patties, about 1 ¼ inches thick
Submerge the patties in the cold water and soak for 30 seconds
Immediately transfer the burgers to the grill
Brush with melted butte
Grill over high (9 mins) , turning once or twice, brushing occasionally with butter
Top the burgers with the cheese during the last minute of grilling and let melt
Spread the Russian dressing on the buns.
Set the lettuce leaves and tomato slices on the bottom halves
Top with the burgers, red onion and bacon

Beef Burgers With Peanut-Chipotle Barbecue Sauce

Ingredients
1 tablespoon vegetable oil, plus more for brushing
1 onion, finely chopped
2 tablespoons minced fresh ginger
2 garlic cloves, minced
1 cup tomato puree
2 tablespoons ketchup
1 tablespoon red wine vinegar
1 tablespoon Worcestershire sauce
1 ½ tablespoons Dijon mustard
2 tablespoons honey
2 tablespoons molasses
3 tablespoons pure ancho chile powder
1 canned Chipotle in adobo, minced
½ cup water
2 tablespoons creamy peanut butter
Salt and freshly ground pepper
4 hamburger buns, split
1 ½ pounds ground beef chuck
½ cup shredded cheddar (3 ounces)
1 scallion, finely chopped
Lettuce and tomato slices, for serving

Directions
In a medium saucepan, heat the 1 tablespoon of oil
Add the onion and ginger, cook over moderate heat, stirring occasionally, until softened,
Add the garlic and cook for 1 minute, stirring
Add tomato puree, ketchup, vinegar, Worcestershire sauce, mustard, honey, molasses, ancho chile powder, Chipotle and water
Bring to a simmer, cooking on low heat, stirring occasionally, until thickened, about 30 minutes. Transfer the sauce to a blender. Add the peanut butter and puree until smooth. Season the barbecue sauce with salt and pepper. Light a grill or preheat a grill pan. Brush the cut sides of the buns with oil and grill until toasted, about 30 seconds. Spread barbecue sauce on the buns. Form the meat into four 1-inch-thick patties and brush with oil. Season with salt and pepper and grill over high heat, turning once, until nearly cooked through, about 5 minutes. Brush the burgers with some of the sauce and grill until lightly glazed, about 2 minutes. Top with the cheddar and scallion. Close the grill and cook just until the cheese is completely melted, about 1 minute. Set the burgers on the buns, top with lettuce and tomato and serve right away.

Chile-Stuffed Cheeseburger

Ingredients
4 Chile peppers. 2 Anaheims and 2 jalapeños
Extra-Virgin Olive Oil
1 large garlic clove, unpeeled
4 ounces shredded Monterey Jack cheese
Salt and freshly ground pepper
1 ½ pounds ground beef
4 kaiser rolls, split
Lettuce leaves, sliced onion and tomato, mayonnaise and ketchup, for dressing

Directions
Light the grill
Rub the chilies with olive oil
Thread the jalapeños and garlic onto a skinny skewer
Grill until uniformly charred
Using tongs, repeat with the Anaheims
Peel the chilies and discard the stems and seeds
Peel the garlic
Chop the chilies and garlic and transfer to a bowl
Fold in the cheese and season with salt and pepper
Cut eight 6-inch squares of wax paper
Divide the beef among the squares
Pat each portion of ground beef into a 5-inch round, a little thicker in the center.
Mound one-fourth of the cheese mixture in the centers of 4 patties
Top with the remaining patties
Press the edges around the periphery in order to seal
Flatten the centers so that the burgers are even
Brush with oil and season with salt and pepper
Brush the cut sides of the Kaiser rolls with oil
Lightly oil the grate
Grill the burgers over a hot fire
Turn once, at about 7 minutes for medium. medium-rare meat
Toast the kaiser rolls.
Place the burgers on top of rolls
Top with lettuce leaves, onion and tomato
Serve with mayonnaise and ketchup

French Onion Dip Burgers

Ingredients

3 tablespoons butter
5 onions, 4 of them thinly sliced and 1 merely peeled
1 bay leaf
Sea salt and pepper
½ teaspoon ground thyme
1 cup beef consomme
1 ½ cups sour cream
2 pounds ground beef sirloin
About ¼ cup Worcestershire sauce (eyeball it)
A handful flat-leaf parsley, finely chopped
EVOO, for drizzling
6 Brioche buns, split
36 good-quality ridged or thick-cut potato chips (cooked in olive oil)
Sliced sweet pickles

Directions

Heat the butter in a large skillet over medium heat
Add the sliced onions and bay leaf
Season with salt, pepper and thyme
Cook, stirring occasionally, until deep caramel and very soft, about 35 minutes
Deglaze with the beef consomme
Cook until almost all of the liquid is absorbed
Let cool
Discard the bay leaf
Stir in the sour cream
Preheat a griddle or large cast-iron skillet over medium-high heat
Season the beef with the Worcestershire, salt (for a crusty coating) and pepper
Grate 4 Tblsp of the peeled onion over the meat
Flavor it and keep the burgers moist
Add the parsley.
Mix the meat, being careful not to overwork it to the point of toughness
Form 6 patties that are thinner at the center than at their edges
Drizzle with EVOO
Cook, turning once, for 6 to 8 minutes for pink centers
Serve the burgers on the buns, topped with the sauce, potato chips and pickles

Wellington Burgers

Ingredients

1 ½ pounds ground sirloin
1 shallot, finely chopped
2. 3 tablespoons finely chopped fresh parsley
1 tablespoon Worcestershire sauce (eyeball it)
Salt and freshly ground pepper
Extra-virgin olive oil , for drizzling
3 tablespoons butter
½ pound either Cremini or white mushrooms, sliced
¼ cup dry sherry
2 tablespoons Dijon mustard
4 eggy rolls, split and toasted, or 8 thick slices Challah bread, toasted
1 small bunch watercress, chopped
½ cup chopped cornichons or baby gherkin pickles
½ pound truffle mousse pate

Directions

In a bowl, mix together ground sirloin, shallot, parsley and Worcestershire sauce
Season with salt and pepper
Score the meat into 4 equal portions
Form into large patties
Heat a drizzle of EVOO in a large nonstick skillet over medium-high heat
When the pan is smoking hot, add the patties
Cook for 4 minutes on each side for medium rare, 6 minutes for medium well
Place a medium skillet over medium heat
Melt 2 tablespoons butter in a drizzle of EVOO,
Add the mushrooms and cook until tender, about 6 minutes
Pour in the sherry and let it cook off, about 30 seconds
Season the mushrooms with salt and pepper and remove from the heat
Stir together the mustard and remaining tablespoon butter
Spread the Dijon butter liberally on the bun bottoms
Top with watercress, a burger patty, a pile of mushrooms and a chopped cornichons
Spread the mousse pate on the bun tops and set them into place

Club Burger Sliders With Avocado-Ranch Dressing

Ingredients
Extra-virgin olive oil (EVOO) or vegetable oil, for drizzling
6 slices center-cut bacon, chopped
2 pounds ground beef
1 small onion
1 tablespoon hot sauce
2 tablespoons poultry seasoning
Salt and pepper
1 Hass avocado
1 cup sour cream
Juice of 1 lemon
1 clove garlic, grated or finely chopped
A small handful each of fresh chives, dill, and flat-leaf parsley , all finely chopped
16 slices good-quality white or whole wheat bread
Bibb or butter lettuce leaves, for serving
2 plum or vine-ripened tomatoes, thinly sliced

Directions
Preheat a cast iron skillet to medium high
Add a drizzle of EVOO and the bacon to the pan
Cook until crisp, about 5 minutes
Drain on paper towels to cool, and drain
Chop the bacon
Place the ground beef in a large bowl
Grate the onion on top of the beef, yielding 3 to 4 tablespoons of onion juice
Add the hot sauce, poultry seasoning, salt and lots of pepper
Add the chopped bacon to mix and form 8 slider patties, about 2 ½ to 3 inches wide
Drizzle with EVOO.
Cook turning once, until cooked through, 8 to 10 minutes
Place the avocado in a food processor
Add sour cream, lemon juice, garlic, chives, dill and parsley
Season with salt & pepper
Process into a smooth, thick sauce
Using a 3-inch round cookie cutter, cut out rounds of bread
Arrange the bread on a baking sheet and toast under a broiler
Serve bacon-turkey sliders with the lettuce, tomatoes and avocado-ranch sauce between the toasts.

Apple-Cheddar Burgers

Ingredients

2 pounds ground beef
4 scallions, finely chopped
1/3 cup chopped flat-leaf parsley (a generous handful)
1 tablespoon grill seasoning
2 tablespoons extra-virgin olive oil (EVOO)
1 apple, such as granny smith, cut into 12 slices
8 slices extra-sharp cheddar cheese
¼ cup whole-berry cranberry sauce
2 tablespoons grainy mustard
4 sandwich-size English muffins, split and toasted
8 leaves red- or green-leaf lettuce

Directions

Combine ground beef, scallions, parsley, grill seasoning and grill seasoning
Form into 4 patties, press your thumb into the center to prevent bulging
In a large skillet, heat the EVOO, 2 turns of the pan, over medium-high heat
Add the patties
Cook for 6 minutes per side, for medium.
Top each patty with 3 apple slices and 2 cheese slices
Tent the pan with aluminum foil and cook until the cheese melts, 1 to 2 minutes
Mix together the cranberry sauce and mustard
Slather the sauce on the muffin tops
Pile 2 lettuce leaves on each muffin bottom
Top with the patties and set the muffin tops into place

Meat Lovers' Burger

Ingredients

2 ripe plum tomatoes sliced ½ inch thick
Sprinkle of oregano
Salt and pepper
EVOO, for drizzling
¼ pound pancetta, speck or bacon, finely diced
1 pound ground beef sirloin
2 large cloves garlic minced or grated
A handful flat-leaf parsley, finely chopped
About 1/8 pound coarsely chopped salami, soppressata or ham
¼ pound ham, prosciutto or prosciutto cotto ends
4 thick deli slices provolone cheese
4 crusty rolls, split
A handful arugula leaves
A handful basil leaves, torn
Thinly-sliced red onion

Directions

Heat the oven to 350 degrees .
Arrange tomatoes on a cooling rack over a baking sheet
Season with oregano, salt and pepper
Drizzle with EVOO
Roast for about 40 minutes to tart them up
Brown the pancetta (or speck or bacon) in a bit of EVOO and let cool
Place beef and pancetta in a mixing bowl
Add the garlic, parsley, along with a little salt and lots of pepper
Grind the salami and ham in the food processor into fine bits
Add the mix to the ground beef
Form the meat blend into 4 patties,.
Drizzle the meat with EVOO
Cook in a skillet over medium-high heat for 8 minutes for medium, flipping occasionally
Top with the cheese and melt
Serve on the rolls
Top with the oven-roasted tomatoes, arugula, basil, red onion and a drizzle of EVOO

Lasagna Burgers

Ingredients
1 ½ pounds ground beef, pork and veal mix
Salt and pepper
2 tablespoons extra-virgin olive oil
1 small onion, finely chopped
2 cloves garlic, chopped
1 14 ½ ounce can Italian crushed tomatoes
1 handful basil leaves, either shredded or torn
2 tablespoons butter
2 tablespoons flour
1 cup milk
A few grates of nutmeg
½ cup Ricotta cheese
¼ cup Parmigiano-Reggiano cheese
4 hamburger or ciabatta rolls

Directions
In a large bowl, season the meat with plenty of salt and pepper
Form into 4 patties
Drizzle with EVOO
In a saucepan, heat 2 tablespoons EVOO, 2 turns of the pan, over medium heat
Add the onion
Cook until softened, about 5 minutes
Add the garlic and cook for 2 minutes more
Stir in the tomatoes and season with salt and pepper.
Lower the heat and simmer for 5 minutes
Stir in the basil.
In large skillet, heat a drizzle of EVOO over medium-high heat
Add the patties and cook, turning once, until medium-rare, from 7 to 8 minutes
While the patties are cooking, melt the butter in a small saucepan over medium heat
Whisk in the flour for 1 minute
Then whisk in the milk
Season with salt, pepper and the nutmeg
Cook until thickened, about 5 minutes
Stir in the ricotta and Parmigiano-Reggiano cheeses
Spoon red sauce on the roll bottoms
Top with the patties.
Dollop the cheese sauce onto the patties and set in place the roll tops

Double-Bacon Burgers
With Maple-Worcestershire Onions

Ingredients
12 slices good-quality smoky bacon
EVOO, for drizzling
2 tablespoons butter
1 large onion, chopped or thinly sliced
Coarse salt and coarse black pepper
½ cup cloudy apple cider
¼ cup dark amber maple syrup
3 tablespoons Worcestershire sauce
1 ½ pounds ground beef sirloin
2 tablespoons grainy Dijon mustard
8 large, thin slices Gruyere or sharp cheddar
4 Brioche buns, split

Directions
Preheat the oven. 375 degrees
Arrange eight slices of bacon on a broiler pan and bake until crisp, 12 to 15 minutes
Finely chop the remaining bacon
In a skillet, heat a drizzle of EVOO over medium-high heat
Add the butter to melt it
Add the onion
Season with salt and pepper
Cook until softened, about 15 minutes
Add the cider, maple syrup and Worcestershire sauce
Simmer at a rapid ,but controlled bubble, stirring frequently, for 8 to 10 minutes
Combine the beef, chopped bacon, mustard and a lot of pepper
Form into 4 patties thinner at the center than at their edges, for more even cooking
Drizzle with EVOO and season with salt
Preheat a cast-iron skillet over medium-high heat
Add the burgers and cook for 5 minutes on the first side
Flip and cook for 3 to 4 minutes on the other side for medium doneness
In the last minute or so, top each burger with 2 slices of cheese to melt
Serve the burgers on the buns, topped with 2 slices of crisp bacon and maple onions.

Nacho Slider Burgers

Ingredients

1 tablespoon tomato paste
1 15 ounce can lard-free spicy refried beans
1 ½ pounds ground sirloin
¼ cup grated onion
2 large cloves garlic, grated or finely chopped
1 tablespoon ancho or other medium-heat chile powder
½ tablespoon ground cumin
½ tablespoon ground coriander
½ tablespoon sweet smoked paprika or sweet paprika
Salt and pepper
Extra-virgin olive oil or vegetable oil, for drizzling
24 Tortilla chips
2 cups shredded yellow sharp cheddar, smoked cheddar or pepper jack cheese
1 heart romaine lettuce or ½ head iceberg lettuce, shredded
2 plum tomatoes, seeded and chopped
Pickled sliced jalapeño chile rings, drained, for serving

Directions

In a medium saucepan, bring about ½ cup water to a rolling boil
In a small cup, mix the tomato paste with a few spoonfuls of the boiling water to thin it
Add the refried beans to the pan, stirring with the water in the pan.
Lower the heat and keep the beans warm
Place the ground sirloin in a bowl
Add reconstituted tomato paste, onion, garlic, chile powder, cumin, coriander & paprika
Season with salt and pepper
Form the meat into eight small patties that are thinner at the center than at their edges
Heat a griddle or skillet over medium-high heat
Drizzle the patties with EVOO
Pace the patties on the griddle and cook for a couple of minutes on each side.
Position a rack in the upper third of the oven and preheat the broiler.
Place the burgers on a rack-covered baking sheet
Top each burger with about two tablespoons beans
Spread 3 chips with some of the remaining refried beans and pile on a burger
Repeat with the remaining chips, beans and sliders
Top the chips with the cheese and broil for a minute. melt
Scatter the lettuce on plates or a platter and top with the sliders, tomatoes and pickled jalapeños

Worcestershire Burgers
with Swiss Cheese, Mushrooms & Ranch Dressing

Ingredients
1 ½ pounds ground beef chuck
About ¼ cup Worcestershire sauce
3 tablespoons grated onion
coarse salt and pepper
1 tablespoon vegetable oil
4 deli slices (not too thin) Emmentaler cheese
3 tablespoons butter
1 pound white mushrooms, slices
1 shallot, finely chopped
1/3 cup dry sherry
1 cup sour cream
¼ to 1/3 cup buttermilk
¼ cup finely chopped dill, parsley, chives and thyme
1 tablespoon fresh lemon juice
1 teaspoon hot sauce
1 clove garlic, grated
4 Brioche or other soft rolls, split

Directions
Preheat a cast-iron skillet or griddle pan over medium-high heat
Combine the chuck, Worcestershire, onion, salt and lots of pepper
Form into 4 patties thinner at the center and thicker at the edges for even cooking
Add the oil to the hot pan
Add the patties
Cook, turning once, for 8 to 10 minutes for medium-rare
During the last 2 minutes cooking, top the patties with cheese, folded to fit the burgers
In a separate skillet, melt the butter over medium heat
Add the mushrooms and cook until browned, about 12 minutes
Add the shallot, season with salt and pepper and cook for 2 to 3 minutes more.
Deglaze the pan with the sherry and remove from the heat
In a bowl, stir together sour cream, buttermilk, herbs, lemon juice, hot sauce and garlic
Season with salt and pepper
Put the cheeseburgers on the roll bottoms
Top with the mushrooms
Slather the roll tops with the dressing

Meatloaf Burgers

Ingredients

4 tablespoons butter
1 small McIntosh apple, peeled and finely chopped
1 small onion, finely chopped
1 small rib celery, finely chopped
Salt and pepper
1/3 cup plain breadcrumbs
1 pound ground beef
1 large egg
¼ cup chopped flat-leaf parsley
2 tablespoons Dijon mustard
2 teaspoons poultry seasoning
Extra-virgin olive oil (EVOO), for drizzling
Sliced sharp white cheddar, for topping
1/3 cup whole-berry cranberry sauce
3 tablespoons sour cream
2 tablespoons chopped chives
4 large sandwich-size sourdough English muffins, split and toasted
4 thin slices red onion
4 leaves red-leaf or red romaine lettuce

Directions

Heat a large skillet over medium heat
Add the butter.
Melt the butter, then add the apple, onion and celery
Season with salt and pepper
Cover and cook until softened, 3 to 4 minutes
Stir in the breadcrumbs
Transfer to a bowl to cool
Reserve the skillet
Mix in beef, egg, parsley, mustard and poultry seasoning season with salt and pepper
Form into four, 4-inch diameter patties
Wipe out the reserved skillet and add a liberal drizzle of EVOO
Warm it over medium-high heat
Add the patties and cook, turning once, until cooked through, 8 to 10 minutes
Top with the cheddar during the last minute
In a small bowl, mix the cranberry sauce, sour cream and chives
Serve patties on English muffins with onion, lettuce and cranberry-sour cream sauce

Pear Burger

Ingredients
2 pounds ground beef
4 scallions, white parts only, finely chopped
2 tablespoons Dijon mustard
1 Lemon, its grated peel and juice
1 tablespoon Fresh thyme chopped
1 Bartlett pear , ripe, cut lengthwise into 8 slices
½ cup Dry white wine
1 tablespoon EVOO
2 cups Sharp white cheddar cheese, shredded
4 tablespoons hot pepper jelly or jalapeño jelly
4 extra-large English muffins, split and toasted

Directions
In a medium bowl, combine the ground beef, scallions, mustard, lemon peel and thyme
Season with salt and pepper.
Shape into four, ¾-inch-thick patties.
In a skillet, add pear slices, wine, lemon juice and just enough water to cover the pear
Bring to a boil
Then lower the heat
Simmer until the pear softens, about 10 minutes.
Using a slotted spoon, transfer the pear slices to a plate
In a large nonstick skillet, heat the EVOO, 1 turn of the pan, over medium heat
Add the patties and cook, turning once, for 12 minutes
Top with the cheese and pear slices
Tent the pan with foil and cook until the cheese is melted, 2 minutes
Spread 1 tablespoon hot pepper jelly on each English muffin bottom
Top with a patty and the English muffin top

Cabin in the Woods Burgers
With Bacon & Eggs

Ingredients
½ pound thick-cut bacon or black-pepper bacon
¼ cup dark amber maple syrup
1 ½ pounds coarsely ground beef chuck
3 tablespoons Worcestershire sauce
3 tablespoons grated onion
2 tablespoons grainy Dijon mustard
Coarse salt and black pepper
EVOO or vegetable oil for drizzling
½ pound sliced extra-sharp white cheddar, for topping
melted butter, for frying eggs and basting burger rolls
4 Organic eggs
4 seed-topped or onion burger rolls, split

Directions
Preheat the oven to 400 degrees F
Bake bacon on broiler or baking sheet until fat is partially rendered, about 15 minutes
Baste the bacon with the maple syrup
Bake until crisp, 5 to 6 minutes
Heat a cast-iron skillet over medium-high heat
Combine the beef, Worcestershire and onion
Grate the onion over the bowl so the juices dribble into the meat
Stir in the mustard
Season with salt and lots of pepper
Form into 4 patties that are thinner at the center and thicker at their edges
Drizzle the patties with oil
Cook, flipping once, until a nice crust forms, about 7 minutes.
Top with the cheese and cook for about 2 minutes to melt
Brush a medium heat skillet with melted butter
Add the eggs and fry
Toast the buns, basting with melted butter.
Top the bun bottoms with a burger, bacon, egg and a bun top

Big Beef Burgers With Crunchy Sour Cream Onions

Ingredients
(Sour Cream Onion Rings)
Vegetable oil, for frying
1 ½ cups buttermilk
½ cup sour cream
1 yellow onion, cut into one-inch-thick slices, separated into rings
1 ½ cups flour
¼ cup finely chopped chives or scallion greens
Salt and coarse black pepper
(Burgers)
2 pounds coarse-ground sirloin beef
¼ cup Worcestershire sauce
Salt and coarse black pepper
EVOO, for drizzling
Brioche rolls or other burger rolls of choice
Chopped crisp lettuce such as iceberg or Romaine heart
(Red Ranch Dressing)
½ cup buttermilk
½ cup sour cream
¼ cup organic or low-sodium ketchup
1 large clove garlic, grated or pasted
3 to 4 tablespoons finely chopped mixed fresh herbs (chives and parsley)
1 tablespoon fresh lemon juice
Salt and coarse black pepper
Hot sauce, to taste

Directions
(For the onion rings) Heat a few inches of vegetable oil in a pot over medium-high heat. Combine 1 ½ cups buttermilk and ½ cup sour cream in a bowl. Add the onion rings. Soak for a few minutes. On a plate, toss the flour with the chives
Season generously with salt and pepper. First, double-dip the onion rings in the liquid followed by the flour. Fry a few rings at a time in the hot oil, turning once, until deep golden, about 4 minutes .Transfer to a rack to cool.
(For the burgers) Combine the beef, Worcestershire, lots of pepper and a little salt
Form 4 large or 12 slider-size patties. Coat with EVOO. Heat a large skillet or griddle to medium-high. Add the burgers and cook. Turn once 8 to 10 minutes for big burgers, 4 to 6 minutes for sliders. While the burgers cook, make the dressing. In a small bowl, combine ½ cup each buttermilk and sour cream, the ketchup, garlic, herbs and lemon juice; season with salt, pepper and hot sauce. Layer the rolls with the burgers, ranch dressing, lettuce and onion rings.

Garlic-Sherry Burgers w/ Stilton & Pub Browns & Horseradish Sauce

Ingredients
1 cup dry sherry
EVOO, for drizzling
5 slices good-quality bacon, sliced crosswise into 1-inch pieces
1 ½. 2 pounds baking potatoes
Coarse salt and black pepper
1 1/3 pounds ground beef (15-20% fat)
¼ cup finely chopped flat-leaf parsley
About 3 Tblsp Worcestershire sauce
4 cloves garlic, grated or pasted
2 large shallots, halved and thinly sliced
12 ounces Stilton or other blue cheese, crumbled
Upland cress or watercress leaves, for garnish
4 Brioche rolls, split
Bread-and-butter pickle slices, for garnish
1 cup sour cream
Splash of heavy cream or half-and-half
2 tablespoons prepared horseradish
3 tablespoons finely chopped fresh chives

Directions
Place the sherry in a medium pot and bring to a boil. Then lower the heat to a simmer and reduce to about 1/3 cup, about 10 minutes. reheat a large cast-iron skillet or griddle to medium-high heat. Heat another large skillet over medium-high heat with a drizzle of EVOO. Scatter the bacon in the pan and brown. Then transfer to a paper-towel-lined plate to drain off the grease. Do leave the drippings in the pan to reserve. Peel the potatoes and halve lengthwise. Slice each half lengthwise into 4 wedges. Then slice crosswise into thirds (24 pieces per potato). Scatter the potato pieces in the reserved bacon drippings. Season with salt and generously with pepper. Cook to brown, about 5 minutes. Cover the skillet with foil. Lower the heat and steam the potatoes, 6 to 7 minutes. Uncover, raise the heat. medium-high, flip and brown on the other side until deep, deep golden and very crisp, 3 to 4 minutes. While the potatoes are busy working, place the beef in a bowl. Season with salt, parsley, Worcestershire, garlic, lots of pepper and a drizzle of EVOO. Combine, but do not overwork. Shape into an even mound and score into 4 portions. Form the portions into mounds. Place the mounds in the preheated skillet and squash into patties with a spatula. Top with the shallots, pressing them in. Cook the burgers for 4 minutes. Flip and then cook for 4 minutes longer. During the last minute or two of cooking top with the Stilton cheese to melt. Douse with the reduced sherry. Place cress on the roll bottoms. Then set on the burgers, pickles and roll tops. Stir together the sour cream, heavy cream, horseradish, chives, salt and pepper. Serve the burgers with the pub browns topped with the horseradish sauce and bacon bits.

Adirondack Red Wing Burger

Ingredients

2 tablespoons extra-virgin olive oil
1 carrot, finely chopped
1 rib celery with leafy tops, finely chopped
¼ cup finely chopped onion
2 cloves garlic, finely chopped
1 ½ pounds ground beef
2 tablespoons finely chopped fresh dill
1 teaspoon grill seasoning
Salt and pepper
2 tablespoons butter
¼ cup hot pepper sauce
½ cup blue cheese crumbles
4 sandwich-size English muffins, toasted
4 deli slices cheddar cheese
¼ head iceberg lettuce, shredded
¼ cup pickle relish

Directions

In a small skillet, heat 1 tablespoon EVOO, 1 turn of the pan, over medium heat
Add the carrot, celery, onion and garlic and cook until tender, about 5 minutes
Transfer to a bowl and let cool
Reserve the skillet
Mix the ground beef, dill and poultry seasoning into the vegetable mixture
Season with salt and pepper
Form into 4 patties
In the reserved skillet, heat the remaining 1 tablespoon EVOO over medium heat
Add the patties and cook, turning once, until firm, about 12 minutes; transfer. a plate
Add the butter. the skillet. melt, then stir in the hot sauce
Add the patties. the sauce, turning to coat
Top each with some of the blue cheese and a cheddar slice
Tent with foil, turn off the heat and let stand until the cheese is melted
Top each muffin bottom with some lettuce, a patty, some relish and a muffin top

New England Burgers
With the Works

Ingredients
3 tablespoons unsalted butter
1 McIntosh apple cored, quartered and finely chopped
1 small onion, finely chopped
2 celery ribs from the heart, finely chopped
1 teaspoon poultry seasoning
Salt and freshly ground pepper
1 ¼ pounds ground beef
Flat-leaf parsley, finely chopped (a generous handful)
1 tablespoon extra-virgin olive oil (EVOO)
1 cup whole-berry cranberry sauce, either prepared or homemade
1 tablespoon finely grated orange zest
2 scallions, finely chopped
4 sandwich-size English muffins, preferably sourdough, fork-split
8 leaves Bibb lettuce

Directions
In a non-stick skillet, melt 2 tablespoons butter over medium heat
Add the apple, onion and celery
Season with the grill seasoning, and salt and pepper to taste
Cook, stirring occasionally, until the onion is tender, 5 to 6 minutes
Transfer to a bowl and let cool for 5 minutes
Wipe the skillet clean and return it to the stove
Preheat the broiler
Add the beef and parsley to the apple mixture
Season with salt and pepper and combine with a fork
Form into four, 4-inch patties
In the skillet, heat the EVOO, 1 turn of the pan, over medium-high heat
Cook the patties for about 6 minutes per side
Lower the heat for the last 2 to 3 minutes
While the burgers cook, mix the cranberry sauce, orange zest and scallions
Toast the English muffins under the broiler
Remove and lightly spread the remaining one tablespoon of butter
Place the cooked burgers on the buttered English muffin bottoms
Top with lettuce, lots of cranberry relish and the buttered tops

The Gaucho Burger

Ingredients

1 ½ pounds lean ground beef sirloin
½ cup beer
2 cloves garlic, grated or finely chopped
2 tablespoons chili powder
1 tablespoon ground cumin
1 tablespoon ground coriander
1 tablespoon steak seasoning
2 teaspoons Worcestershire sauce
1 red onion, cut into 6 wedges
1/3 cup chopped cilantro
Juice of 1 lime plus 1 teaspoon grated peel
Salt
8 deli slices pepper jack cheese
4 kaiser rolls, preferably cornmeal crusted, split and toasted
Shredded romaine lettuce

Directions

Combine beef, beer, garlic, chili powder, cumin, coriander, seasoning Worcestershire
Shape into 4 patties
Preheat the broiler or outdoor grill

If using a broiler, halve and seed the tomatoes and jalapeños before broiling
On a rimmed baking sheet, broil the tomatoes, jalapeños and red onion,

Turn once, until charred, about 15 minutes
If using an outdoor grill, char the vegetables for 10 minutes
Halve and seed the tomatoes and jalapeños.
Chop the charred veggies
Transfer in a bowl
Add the cilantro, lime juice and lime peel
Season the pico de gallo with salt
Cook the burgers over medium-high heat for 5 minutes on each side for medium-rare, r
During the last few minutes of cooking, melt the cheese over each burger
To serve, layer each roll bottom with lettuce, a burger, a splash of pico de gallo and a
roll top

Ham Burger

Ingredients
1 pound lean ground pork
¾ pound deli-sliced honey-baked ham, coarsely chopped
2 tablespoons pure maple syrup
1 tablespoon grill seasoning
2 teaspoons hot pepper sauce
½ teaspoon dry mustard
2 tablespoons extra-virgin olive oil (EVOO)
4 ½. inch-thick slices fresh pineapple
4 Kaiser rolls, split and toasted
1 cup pineapple or mango chutney
8 red-leaf lettuce leaves
1 red onion, thinly sliced

Directions
Combine the pork, ham, maple syrup, grill seasoning, hot sauce and mustard
Form into four patties
In a large skillet, heat 1 tablespoon EVOO, 1 turn of the pan, over medium-high heat
Add pineapple slices and cook, turning once, until golden, about 5 minutes
Transfer to a plate
In the same skillet, heat 1 tablespoon EVOO, 1 turn of the pan, over med-high heat.
Add the patties and cook, turning once, until cooked through, 8 to 10 minutes
Place 1 patty on each roll bottom
Top with some chutney, lettuce, a pineapple slice, onion and a roll top

Herby's Beef Burger

Ingredients

1 ½ pounds ground beef sirloin
1/3 cup finely chopped flat-leaf parsley (a generous handful)
1/3 cup finely chopped dill (a generous handful)
¼ cup chopped chives
1 tablespoon Worcestershire sauce (eyeball it)
Salt and pepper
1 4 ounce log goat cheese, quartered
Extra-virgin olive oil (EVOO)
1/3 cup sour cream
¼ cup Dijon mustard
3 tablespoons honey
4 crusty whole grain kaiser rolls, split
4 leaves green-leaf lettuce
¼ seedless cucumber, thinly sliced
4 radishes, thinly sliced
4 thin slices red onion

Directions

Preheat a grill or grill pan to medium-high
In a large bowl, combine the beef, parsley, dill, chives and Worcestershire sauce
Season with salt and pepper
Divide the mixture into 4 mounds
Press one piece of cheese in the center of each mound
Form a patty around the cheese
Drizzle the patties with EVOO
Grill for four minutes on each side for medium
Meanwhile, in a small bowl, combine the sour cream, mustard and honey
Season with salt and pepper
Layer each roll bottom with lettuce, cucumber, radish, onion and a burger
Spread honey mustard sauce on the cut side of the bun tops
Serve

Welsh Rarebit Burgers

Ingredients
8 slices bacon
1 ½ pounds lean ground beef
1 shallot, finely chopped
1/3 cup finely chopped parsley
Salt and pepper
Extra-virgin olive oil (EVOO), for drizzling
2 tablespoons butter
2 tablespoons flour
2 tablespoons Worcestershire sauce
1 tablespoon dry or prepared mustard
1 teaspoon hot sauce
¾- 1 cup stout, such as Guinness
1 pound shredded cheddar cheese
8 slices pumpernickel bread
1 small bunch watercress, chopped
4 thick slices beefsteak tomato
Salt-and-vinegar potato chips, for serving

Directions
Preheat the oven to 350 degrees
Bake the bacon on a broiler pan until crisp, 15 minutes
In a bowl, combine the beef, shallot and parsley; season with salt and pepper
Form into 4 patties
In a nonstick skillet, heat a drizzle of EVOO over high heat
Add the patties and cook for 3 minutes on each side for medium-rare
In a large saucepan, melt the butter over medium heat
Whisk in the flour and cook until light brown, 3 minutes
Stir in the Worcestershire sauce, mustard and hot sauce
Whisk in the stout and cook until thickened, 1 to 2 minutes
Lower the heat and stir in the cheese until smooth
Arrange the pumpernickel bread slices on a baking sheet and toast both sides
Pour the sauce over the toasts
Broil until the cheese is bubbly, about 2 minutes
Place a patty on each of the four slices
Cover each with a handful of watercress, crisscross with two bacon slices
Top with a slice of tomato, season with salt and pepper
Cover with the remaining toasts, cheesy side down

Tex-Mex Bacon Cheeseburgers

Ingredients

12 slices good-quality smoky bacon, 4 slices finely chopped and 8 left whole

1 ¼ pounds 80% lean ground beef

3. 4 tablespoons grated onion

2 cloves garlic, finely chopped or grated

2 tablespoons pureed Chipotle in adobo sauce

2 tablespoons Worcestershire sauce

Salt and pepper

Vegetable oil or EVOO, for drizzling

3 tablespoons butter

2 tablespoons flour

1 cup milk

1 ½ cups shredded cheddar

1 14 ounce can diced tomatoes with green chilies, well drained

Rolls &toppings

4 soft burger rolls, split

Crisp yellow corn chips

Chopped onion, tomatoes, cilantro and pickled jalapeño

Directions

Arrange 8 whole bacon slices on a broiler pan

Bake at 375 degrees until crisp, 10 to 12 minutes

Preheat a cast-iron skillet or griddle over medium-high heat

Combine beef, chopped bacon, grated onion, garlic, Chipotle puree and Worcestershire

Season with salt and pepper

Form into 4 patties (thinner at the center)

Drizzle with oil

Grill the burgers for 5 minutes on each side for medium.

(to make the queso sauce)

In a medium saucepan, melt the butter over medium heat.

Whisk in flour for 1 minute, then whisk in the milk.

Stir in the cheese. melt.

Stir in the tomatoes.

Place the burgers on the bun bottoms

Top with the queso sauce, criss-crossed bacon strips, corn chips, & remaining toppings

Serve extra sauce on the side

Double-Decker

Ingredients
½ cup sour cream
¼ cup ketchup
2 tablespoons dill pickle relish
1 tablespoon white wine vinegar
1 teaspoon superfine sugar
Salt and pepper
2 tablespoons EVOO
2 large onions, chopped
Salt and pepper
½ cup beef stock or consomme
2 pounds ground beef
¼ cup Worcestershire sauce
4 cloves garlic, finely chopped
A handful flat-leaf parsley, finely chopped
Coarse salt and coarse pepper
EVOO, for drizzling
½ cup Dijon or grainy Dijon mustard
8 slices Swiss or Comte
4 Brioche or other hamburger buns, split
Sliced bread-and-butter pickles, sliced tomatoes and chopped lettuce, for serving

Directions
Mix the first 5 ingredients
Season with salt and pepper
Heat the EVOO In a skillet over medium heat
Add the onions and season with salt and pepper
Cook until browned, about 15 minutes.
Stir in the stock (or consomme) and cook until tender, 10 to 15 minutes
Combine the beef, Worcestershire sauce, garlic and parsley
Season with coarse salt and pepper
Form into 8 thin patties and drizzle with EVOO
Top each patty with 1 Tblsp mustard.
Add patties to pan (medium-high heat) mustard side up and cook for 4 minutes
Flip, then cook for 2 more minutes.
Top with the cheese to melt in the last minute of cooking
Stack 2 patties with some onions between them on each bun bottom.
Top with the pickles, tomatoes, lettuce, special sauce and bun tops

Spicy Chicken-Fried Hamburgers

Ingredients
Peanut or other vegetable oil, for frying
Coarse salt and pepper
1 tablespoon sweet paprika
1 ½ teaspoons granulated garlic or garlic powder
1 ½ teaspoons granulated onion
1 teaspoon cayenne
1 teaspoon ground cumin
1 ½ pounds ground beef chuck
2 cups flour
4 large eggs
1 ½ cups heavy cream
4 potato rolls, toasted and buttered
Lettuce, tomato, red onion, pickles and honey mustard for topping
¾ cup organic ketchup mixed with 2 Tblsp Worcestershire sauce, or barbecue sauce

Directions
In a deep fryer or Dutch oven, heat the oil. 375 degrees
Combine 1 Tblsp each salt, pepper, the paprika, granulated garlic, onion, cayenne and cumin
Mix half of the spice blend into the beef.
Form 4 thin patties
In a shallow dish, combine the remaining spice blend and the flour
In another dish, whisk the eggs and cream
Coat the burgers: flour, egg, flour, egg, flour
Add 2 burgers at a time. the fryer or Dutch oven
Fry until golden, 4. 5 minutes
Transfer. a rack. drain
On the roll bottoms, layer the burgers, lettuce, tomato, red onion, pickles and ketchup mixture (or barbecue sauce).
Slather honey mustard on the roll top s and set in place

Nota bene: When using a Dutch oven, the cooking oil needs. be at least 2-½ inches deep and 2 inches below the top of the pot.

Patty Melts

Ingredients

1 cup sour cream
¼ cup ketchup
2 tablespoons dill pickle relish
1 tablespoon lemon juice
1 teaspoon hot sauce, such as Tabasco
Salt and pepper
1 ¼ pounds ground beef
3 tablespoons grated onion (grate over the the ground beef to catch the juices)
2 tablespoons finely chopped flat-leaf parsley
1 tablespoon Worcestershire sauce
1 ½ teaspoons ground poultry seasoning; such as Bell's
Coarsely ground salt and pepper
A drizzle of vegetable oil or extra virgin olive oil
1 1-pound rinsed and drained sauerkraut,
8 slice marbled rye or pumpernickel bread
4 tablespoons butter; softened
8 slice Emmentaler
8 slice sharp cheddar
Spicy brown mustard

Directions

In a small bowl, combine all of the dressing ingredients
Heat a griddle pan over medium-high heat.
Combine all of the patty ingredients except for the oil
Form 4 patties
Drizzle the oil on the griddle
Add the patties and cook
Turn once, until cooked through, 8 to 10 minutes
Transfer to a plate
Wipe the griddle clean
Warm the sauerkraut over medium heat
Lightly spread 1 side of each bread slice with the butter
With the buttered sides facing down, build the patty melts
Spread dressing liberally on the unbuttered sides of 4 bread slices
Top with 2 Emmentaler slices, a layer of sauerkraut, a patty and 2 Cheddar slices
Slather mustard on the unbuttered sides of the other 4 bread slices and set in place
Griddle, turning once, until crisp on the outside add the cheese is melted, 6 to 8 minutes

The Pittsburger

Ingredients
2 baking potatoes, cut lengthwise into -inch-thick fries
Cooking spray
Salt and pepper
2 tablespoons butter
2 cloves garlic, minced
2 tablespoons chopped parsley
1/3 cup white wine vinegar
3 tablespoons EVOO
1 tablespoon superfine sugar
½ pound cabbage, shredded
Celery salt
1 cup ketchup, preferably organic or low-sodium
¼ cup balsamic vinegar
1 ½ pounds ground chuck or sirloin
3 tablespoons grated onion
2 tablespoons Worcestershire sauce
8 thin slices provolone
8 slices (1-inch thick)Italian bread

Directions
Preheat the oven to 325 degrees F
Soak the potatoes in salted water for 15 minutes
Drain, pat dry and arrange on a baking sheet
Spray the potatoes with cooking spray and bake for 10 minutes
Season with salt and pepper
Increase the oven temperature to 475 degrees
Bake, turning once, until very crisp and golden-brown all over, about 30 minutes
In a small skillet, melt the butter over medium heat
Add the garlic, then remove from the heat and stir in the parsley
Pour over the baked fries
Whisk the white wine vinegar, EVOO and sugar
Add the cabbage and season with celery salt and pepper, toss
Stir together the ketchup and balsamic vinegar
Combine the beef, onion and Worcestershire sauce and season with salt and black pepper
Form 4 patties, thinner at the center and thicker at the edges for more even cooking
Put in the skillet and cook, flipping once, for 8 minutes for medium rare
Top each burger with 2 slices of cheese and let melt
Layer the burgers between the bread slices, topped with the slaw, fries and sauce.

Tenderloin Burgers With Horseradish Sauce

Ingredients
1 ½ pounds beef tenderloin, cubed
¼ cup very finely chopped flat-leaf parsley
¼ cup grated onion
1 large egg yolk, beaten
kosher salt and coarse pepper
2 tablespoons butter
Sliced mozzarella or mild cheddar (optional)
4 Brioche burger rolls, split and lightly toasted
Horseradish Sauce
Ketchup, for serving

Directions
Using a grinder or pulsing in a food processor, coarsely grind the tenderloin meat
Transfer to a bowl
Add the parsley, onion, egg yolk and salt and pepper to taste
Form 4 patties
Heat a griddle or large, heavy skillet over medium-high heat
Add the butter
When it foams, add the burgers
Cook 6 to 8 minutes for rare, turning once
For cheeseburgers, top with the cheese during the last two minutes of cooking
Serve the burgers on the rolls
Top with the horseradish sauce and ketchup

Monte Cristo Burger

Ingredients
(Toasts)
4 eggs
½ cup freshly grated Parmigiano-Reggiano
½ lemon, juiced
Salt and pepper
EVOO and butter, for griddling
8 slices Italian bread

(Burgers)
1 ½ pounds ground beef
½ cup flat-leaf parsley, finely chopped
3 tablespoons capers, chopped
1 lemon, zested and juiced
1 large shallot, finely chopped
4 cloves garlic, finely chopped
½ teaspoon salt
½ teaspoon pepper
2 tablespoons EVOO
6 cups baby spinach

Directions
Preheat the oven to 200 degrees
Heat a griddle over medium
In a bowl, beat the eggs with the cheese and lemon juice
Season with salt and pepper
Drizzle the griddle with EVOO, then melt a dab of butter into the oil
Coat the bread in the egg mixture and cook until golden, 3 minutes per side
Transfer the toasts to a plate and keep warm in the oven
Increase the heat to medium-high
Combine the meat parsley, capers, lemon zest, shallot, garlic, salt and pepper.
Form the mixture into 4 patties
Drizzle the griddle with the EVOO
Add the patties and cook until browned and cooked through, 6 to 7 minutes per side
Drizzle the burgers with the lemon juice, divide among four toasts
Add the spinach to the griddle
Toss until wilted, then season
Pile the spinach on the burgers and top with the remaining toasts

Bloody Bull Burgers With Crunchy Ketchup

Ingredients

¼ cup Worcestershire sauce
3 tablespoons tomato pasta
3 tablespoons freshly grated horseradish or 2 Tblsp prepared horseradish
2 tablespoons finely chopped flat-leaf parsley
1 tablespoon fresh lemon juice (omit if using prepared horseradish)
2 pounds ground bison or sirloin
1 tablespoon coarse black pepper
1 teaspoon kosher salt
1 teaspoon celery salt
¾ cup ketchup, preferably organic
¼ cup your favorite steak sauce
2 tablespoons very finely chopped celery ribs and leaves
1 tablespoon Tabasco
2 teaspoons EVOO
6 onion rolls, split and lightly toasted
Romaine leaves
Beefsteak tomato slices
Thinly sliced onions
Pimiento-stuffed olives (optional)
Cocktail onions (optional)

Directions

Combine the Worcestershire sauce, tomato paste, horseradish, parsley and lemon juice
Add the meat, pepper, kosher salt and celery salt
Using your hands, mix
Combine
Form into 6 patties (thinner at the center for even cooking)
Mix the ketchup,steak sauce, celery and Tabasco to add crunch to the ketchup.
In a cast-iron skillet or on a griddle pan, heat the EVOO over medium-high.
Cook the patties, turning once, about 8 minutes for medium-rare.
Divide the patties among the roll bottoms.
Top with the lettuce, tomato, onion, crunchy ketchup and roll tops
Garnish the burgers with olives and onions, skewered on toothpicks

Creamed-Spinach Knife & Fork Burgers

Ingredients

2 tablespoons EVOO or canola oil

1 small onion, finely chopped

2 or 3 cloves of garlic, grated

3 ounces cream cheese

1/3 cup heavy cream

A pinch freshly grated or ground nutmeg

Salt and pepper

1 16 ounce bag frozen chopped organic spinach, thawed and squeezed dry

½ to ¾ cup grated Parmigiano-Reggiano

2 pounds ground sirloin

¼ cup Worcestershire sauce

1 tablespoon coarse black pepper

Kosher salt

½ cup beef stock or consomme

4 ¾-inch-thick slices good-quality white bread, toasted and buttered

Store-bought french-fried onions

Directions

In a large skillet, heat EVOO, two turns of the pan, over medium

Add the onion and cook until softened, 5 to 7 minutes

Add the garlic and stir 1 minute

Add the cream cheese

Stir until melted

Add the cream and nutmeg

Season with salt and pepper.

Add the spinach and stir until heated through, about 3 minutes.

Stir in the cheese

Combine the sirloin, Worcestershire and black pepper

Season with kosher salt

Form 4 large patties (thinner at the center for even cooking).

Heat a grill pan or cast-iron skillet over medium-high

Cook the burgers, turning once, about 8 minutes for medium-rare.

Transfer the burgers to a plate.

Add the stock to the skillet

Cook, stirring, until reduced slightly, 2 to 3 minutes.

Divide the toast among 4 plates and top with the burgers

Drizzle each burger with sauce from the skillet, then top with creamed spinach, onions

Brunch Burgers

Ingredients

12 slices peppered bacon
½ cup (packed) dark brown sugar
3 tablespoons pure maple syrup, divided
¾ pound ground beef
¾ pound ground pork
1 teaspoon fennel seeds
1 teaspoon granulated garlic
1 teaspoon granulated onion
1 teaspoon ground sage
1 teaspoon black pepper
1 teaspoon kosher salt
¼ teaspoon cayenne pepper
1 tablespoon canola or vegetable oil
4 thick slices sharp cheddar or Cooper Sharp American cheese
4 medium eggs
3 tablespoons soft butter
1 tablespoon whole-grain mustard
4 sandwich-size English muffins, toasted

Directions

Arrange a rack in the center of the oven
Preheat the oven to 375 degrees F
Set a wire rack inside a rimmed baking sheet lined with foil
Place the bacon slices on a cutting board
In a small bowl, mix together the brown sugar and 2 Tblsp maple syrup
Press the brown sugar mixture onto 1 side of the bacon
Transfer the bacon to the wire rack, brown-sugar side up
Bake until crispy, about 30 minutes
Combine the ground beef, ground pork and seasonings
Form into four patties thinner at the center and thicker at the edges for even cooking
In a skillet or griddle pan, heat the oil over medium-high
Cook the patties, turning once, 8 to 10 minutes for medium
Top each patty with one slice of cheese during the last minute or two of cooking.
Transfer the patties. a plate, then cook the eggs over easy
In a small bowl, mix the butter, 1 Tblsp maple syrup and mustard
Spread maple-mustard butter on the English muffins
Divide the patties among the muffin bottoms, top with the bacon, eggs and muffin tops

Sloppy Lasagna Joes

Ingredients
Garlic Rolls
2 tablespoons EVOO
3 tablespoons butter
2 large cloves garlic, finely chopped
1 tablespoon finely chopped fresh parsley
6 ciabatta rolls or sesame semolina rolls, split
2 to 3 tablespoons grated Parmigiano-Reggiano cheese
Sloppy Lasagna Filling
2 tablespoons EVOO
1/8 pound pancetta, finely chopped
1 ¾ pounds ground beef
1 small onion, finely chopped
2 large cloves garlic, finely chopped
½ teaspoon crushed red pepper
2 tablespoons tomato paste
1 cup beef or chicken stock
1 cup Passata or strained tomato puree
½ cup dry white wine or red wine
¼ cup milk
Salt and pepper and few leaves fresh basil, torn
¾ cup fresh cow's-or sheep's-milk ricotta, drained

Directions
In a small pan, heat the EVOO, two turns of the pan, over medium
Melt the butter in the oil. When the butter foams, add garlic, swirl for 1 to 2 minutes
Remove from heat and stir in the parsley
In a hot oven, or under the broiler, lightly toast the rolls
Spread with the garlic butter and then sprinkle with the cheese
Bake or broil until the cheese melts
In a large skillet, heat the EVOO, two turns of the pan, over medium-high heat
Add pancetta and cook, stirring, for 2 minutes
Add beef and cook, breaking it up with a wooden spoon, until browned, five minutes
Add onion, garlic and crushed red pepper and cook, stirring occasionally, five minutes
Add the tomato paste and stir one minute
Stir in the stock, passata, wine and milk,reduce the heat to low and stir in the basil
Simmer until the filling thickens and the flavors meld, 15 to 20 minutes
Season the filling, then spoon onto the roll bottoms. Top with the ricotta and roll tops

Spicy Cheddar Burgers
with Chunky Blue Cheese Aioli

Ingredients

2 pounds ground sirloin or chuck
2 tablespoons Worcestershire sauce
2 tablespoons grainy Dijon mustard
2 tablespoons prepared horseradish
Kosher salt and coarse black pepper
Melted butter, for basting
12 ounces (¾ lb.) sliced sharp white cheddar
6 burger rolls, toasted
Green leaf or butter lettuce
Sliced beefsteak tomatoes
1 Vidalia or other mild sweet onion, thinly sliced
HOMEMADE MAYO
1 organic egg yolk
1 teaspoon Dijon mustard
2 tablespoons fresh lemon juice
2/3 cup grapeseed oil
Sea salt
CHUNKY BLUE CHEESE AIOLI
1 cup Homemade Mayo or store-bought mayo
6 ounces crumbled blue cheese or smoked blue cheese crumbles
2 tablespoons finely chopped flat-leaf parsley
1 tablespoon grainy Dijon mustard
1 large clove garlic, grated or pasted

Directions

Combine the beef, Worcestershire, Dijon and horseradish; season with salt and pepper.
Shape into 6 patties
Cook the meat on a cast-iron skillet over medium-high.
Turn occasionally and baste with melted butter, about eight minutes for medium-rare
Top with slices of cheddar and cover for the last minute until the cheese melts
For the mayo, in a medium bowl, whisk the egg yolk, Dijon and lemon juice
Continuing too whisk, slowly stream in the oil, letting it pour down the sides of the bowl
For the aioli, , mix the mayo, blue cheese, parsley, Dijon and garlic
Divide the cheeseburgers among the roll bottoms
Spread the aioli on the roll tops
Top the burgers with lettuce, tomato, onion and the roll tops

Tex-Mex Bacon Cheeseburger With Chipotle Ketchup

Ingredients
12 slices bacon, 4 slices of which are to be chopped
EVOO, for drizzling
1 small yellow onion, chopped
2 jalapeño chile peppers, chopped
4 cloves garlic, chopped
1 ½ pounds ground beef
1 tablespoon sweet smoked paprika
1 ½ teaspoons ground cumin
1 ½ teaspoons ground coriander
1 tablespoon oregano, preferably Mexican
Salt and pepper
4 slices smoked or sharp cheddar
4 slices pepper jack
4 crusty burger rolls, split and toasted
Lettuce leaves and red onion slices, for serving
Chipotle Ketchup
1 cup tomato sauce
3 tablespoons pureed Chipotle chilies in adobo sauce
2 tablespoons light brown sugar
2 tablespoons vinegar
1 tablespoon Worcestershire sauce

Directions
Preheat the oven to 400 degrees F
Place 8 whole slices of bacon on a broiler pan
Bake in the oven until crisp, about 15 minutes
In a skillet, heat a drizzle of EVOO over medium-high heat
Add the chopped bacon and cook until crisp, about 5 minutes
Transfer to paper towels, drain, leaving two Tblsp of the bacon fat in the pan
Add yellow onion, jalapeño and garlic and cook until softened, 7 to 8 minutes
Combine beef, chopped bacon, onion mixture, paprika, cumin, coriander and oregano
Season with salt and pepper. Form into 4 patties and add to the skillet
Cook over medium-high heat, turning once, for 8 minutes for medium
During the last minute or two of cooking, add one slice of each cheese on top of a patty
Layer each roll bottom w/burger, 2 bacon slices, lettuce, red onion, Chipotle Ketchup
Combine all of the ingredients, simmer over low heat until thickened, about 20 minutes

Pimento Cheese Patty Melts with Bacon

Ingredients
8 slices smoky bacon
1 ½ pounds ground beef
Coarse salt and pepper
2 tablespoons Worcestershire sauce
2 tablespoons finely chopped fresh parsley
2 tablespoons grated onion
1 tablespoon EVOO or vegetable oil
½ pound sharp yellow cheddar, grated
1 4 ounce jar chopped pimientos, drained
1 3 ounce package cream cheese
About ¼ cup mayonnaise
2 teaspoons hot sauce, such as Frank's RedHot
1 teaspoon sweet paprika
2 cloves garlic, minced or grated
Softened butter
8 slices of good-quality white bread

Directions
Preheat the oven to 375 degrees F
Bake the bacon on a broiler pan until crisp, about 15 minutes
In a large bowl, season the beef with salt and pepper
Mix in the Worcestershire, parsley and onion
Form four large patties (thinner in the middle for even cooking)
In a large skillet or cast-iron griddle, heat the EVOO over medium-high heat
Put the patties in the skillet.
Cook, turning once, for about eight minutes for medium-rare
Transfer to a plate.
With an electric mixer, combine cheddar, pimientos, cream cheese, mayo, hot sauce, paprika and garlic until well mixed, one to two minutes

Reheat the skillet or griddle over medium heat
Butter one side of each bread slice, placing buttered side down on a work surface
Spread with cheese mixture.
Top each slice with a burger, two pieces of bacon and another bread slice
Griddle until golden and the cheese is melted

Philly Burgers

Ingredients

2 ½ pounds ground sirloin
1/3 cup Worcestershire sauce
¼ cup finely chopped flat-leaf parsley
6 cloves garlic, minced or grated
2 teaspoons chopped fresh oregano, or 1 tsp dried oregano
Kosher salt and coarse black pepper
2 tablespoons EVOO
2 onions, halved and thinly sliced
3 cubanelle peppers-halved, seeded and thinly sliced
1 fresh red or green chile pepper, seeded and thinly sliced, or 1 tsp crushed red pepper
1 cup beef or veal stock
16 slices deli-cut Provolone cheese
8 crusty rolls, split and lightly toasted

Directions

Combine the beef, Worcestershire sauce, parsley, garlic, oregano, salt and pepper
Place in the refrigerator until chilled, to meld flavors
Heat 2 Tblsp EVOO in a skillet, 2 turns of the pan, over medium-high heat
Add the onions, season with salt and pepper and cook for 5 minutes
Add the Cubanelle peppers and chile pepper (or crushed red pepper)
Cook 7 to 8 minutes to soften
Keep the onions and peppers moist and saucy by adding the stock a little bit at a time.
Bring the meat to room temperature
Form 6 to 8 patties thinner at the center than at the edges, for more even cooking
Drizzle with EVOO
On a grill or large skillet , cook the patties over medium-high heat to desired doneness
During the last minute of cooking, melt two slices of provolone over each patty
Serve burgers on the toasted rolls topped with the saucy peppers and onions

Saltimbocca Burgers

Ingredients

4 ounces Gorgonzola dolce
4 tablespoons butter, softened
2 pounds ground veal or chicken
12 sage leaves, chopped
2 cloves garlic, pasted or grated
1 tablespoon lemon zest
Salt and pepper
EVOO, for drizzling
4 slices prosciutto di Parma, folded in half crosswise
4 ciabatta, or other crusty rolls, split
Spinach (optional)

Directions

Preheat the broiler
Combine the cheese and butter
Combine the meat with the sage, garlic and lemon zest; season with salt and pepper
Form into four patties
Drizzle the patties with EVOO
On a griddle pan or large skillet, cook the patties over medium- high heat
Turning occasionally, cook from 10 to 12 minutes
Transfer the burgers to a plate
Add prosciutto to the skillet
Cook until crisp on both sides, turning once, 2 minutes
Transfer the prosciutto to a plate
Toast the rolls under the broiler
Slather with the Gorgonzola butter
In the same skillet, wilt the spinach over medium-high heat
Place spinach on each roll bottom.
Top with the patties, prosciutto and roll tops

Cobb-Style Burgers

Ingredients
8 sliced smoky bacon
4 ounces blue cheese
6 tablespoons butter, softened
1 ½ pounds ground sirloin
2 tablespoons Worcestershire sauce
2 tablespoons finely chopped fresh parsley
Salt and coarse black pepper
EVOO or vegetable oil, for drizzling
4 slices ripe, beefsteak tomato
1 ripe avocado, sliced
1 tablespoon fresh lemon juice
4 Brioche hamburger rolls, split and toasted
4 leaves Romaine lettuce, stemmed
4 thinly-sliced red onions

Directions
Preheat the oven to 375 degrees
Arrange the bacon on a broiler pan, or rack, set over a foil-lined baking sheet
Bake until crisp, 15 to 17 minutes
Preheat a cast-iron or other heavy skillet over medium-high heat
Stir together the blue cheese and butter
Combine ground meat, Worcestershire, parsley, salt and copious pepper
Form into 4 patties
Drizzle the hot pan with EVOO
Add the patties and cook, turning once, for 8 minutes for medium-rare beef
Season the tomato with salt and pepper
Dress the avocado with the lemon juice
Place the burgers on the bun bottoms and slather with the blue cheese butter
Layer with the bacon, lettuce, tomato, avocado, onion and bun tops

Grilled, Brie-Stuffed Burgers
With Bacon

Ingredients
8 slices of bacon
1 pound lean ground beef
6 ounces Brie (rind removed), cut into 4 pieces
EVOO, for brushing
Salt and pepper
4 hamburger buns, split
Mayonnaise, tomato and lettuce, for serving

Directions
Preheat a grill in two parts: low and medium heat.
Cover
Grill the bacon over low heat, turning halfway through, until crisp, 10 minutes
Let drain.
Divide the beef into quarters.
Enclose a piece of cheese in each quarter
Pat into four, four-inch patties.
Brush with EVOO and season with salt and pepper
Cover and grill the patties over medium heat, turning once, until browned
Grill the buns over low heat until toasted, two minutes.
Assemble the burgers on the buns replete with the mayo, tomato, lettuce and bacon

Inside-Out Cheeseburgers

Ingredients
½ cup crumbled blue cheese (2. 3 ounces)
2 ounces cream cheese
2 tablespoons chopped flat-leaf parsley
1 ½ pounds ground beef
Salt and pepper
2 tablespoons vegetable oil
2 tablespoons butter
4 hamburger buns, split and toasted
Lettuce, onion slices and condiments

Directions
Mash together the blue cheese and cream cheese with a fork until smooth
Stir in the parsley
Divide the mixture into 4 disks about 1 ½ inches across
Cover tightly with plastic wrap and refrigerate for at least 20 minutes
Season the beef with salt and pepper and mix well
Form into 4 equally-sized patties about ¾ inch thick
Form a deep cavity in the center of each beef patty
Place a cheese disk in each cavity and pull the meat together to completely cover cheese
In a large skillet, heat the oil and butter over medium-high heat
Add the burgers and cook about 4 minutes per side for medium
Serve on the buns with the lettuce, onion and condiments

The North Carolina Burger

Ingredients
1 large slice high-quality white sandwich bread (crust removed and discarded, bread chopped into -inch pieces, about ½ cup)
2 tablespoons whole milk
3/4 teaspoon table salt
3/4 teaspoon ground black pepper
1 medium clove garlic minced or pressed (about 1 teaspoon)
2 teaspoons steak sauce
2 tablespoons bacon grease
1 ½ lbs ground chuck
Vegetable oil for cooking grate
6 ounces American or cheddar cheese, sliced
4 hamburger buns or rolls
A&W Chili (recipe follows)
Creamy Coleslaw
Diced onions Mustard

Directions
Preheat grill to very hot. After 15 minutes, scrape the cooking grate clean, coat with oil
Leave primary burner on high, turn other burner(s) to low.
Mash bread and milk in large bowl with fork until homogeneous
Stir in salt, pepper, garlic, steak sauce, and reserved bacon fat
Mix until thoroughly blended.
Break up beef into small pieces over bread mixture
Lightly mix together to form a cohesive mass. Divide meat into 4 equal portions
Gently toss one portion of meat back and forth between hands to form loose ball. Gently flatten into 3/4-inch-thick patty about 4 ½ inches in diameter.
Press center of patty down with fingertips until it is about ½ inch thick, creating a slight depression in each patty. Repeat.
Lightly dip wad of paper towels in vegetable oil; holding wad with tongs, wipe cooking grate. Grill burgers on hot side of grill, covered, until well seared on first side, 2 to 4 minutes. Using wide metal spatula, flip burgers and continue grilling, about 3 minutes for medium-well or 4 minutes for well-done.
Distribute equal portions of cheese on burgers about 2 minutes before they reach desired doneness, covering burgers with disposable aluminum pan to melt cheese. While burgers grill, toast buns on cooler side of grill, rotating as necessary
Serve burgers on toasted buns.
Serve with cheese, chili, onions, Caroline mustard and Cole slaw
Nota bene: Carolinians eat a lot of chili, coleslaw (authentically made with Dukes mayonnaise, and mustard. So it's only logical to place those condiments on a burger.

The California Burger

Ingredients
1 -1 1/1 lbs ground sirloin
4 San Francisco sourdough hamburger buns
8 slices pepper bacon
4 slices American cheese
4 slices sweet onions
4 slices tomatoes
roasted red pepper
1 Avocado
Crispy Romaine lettuce

Directions
Slice the avocado around its circumference
Split in two
Use a spoon to pluck out the pit and to scrape the flesh from the rind
Slice the avocado into strips
Cook the bacon
Separate the ground sirloin into 4 patties
Cook the burger four to five minutes per side on an oiled grill
When just about done, melt a slice of American cheese on each burger
Salt and pepper to taste
Top the burger with lettuce, tomato, onion, guacamole or avocado and bacon
Serve on whole-grain bread with sprouts

Glossary

Brie - Brie is a soft cow's milk cheese named after Brie, the French region from which it originated, roughly corresponding to the modern département of Seine-et-Marne. It is pale in color with a slight grayish tinge beneath a rind of white mold. The rind is edible. Its flavor depends largely upon the ingredients used and manufacturing methods.

Brioche - Is a pastry of French origin , similar to a highly enriched bread, whose high egg and butter content lend it a rich and tender crumb. It is light and slightly puffy, more or less fine, depending on the proportion of butter and eggs. Its dark, golden, and flaky crust, is often accentuated by an egg wash applied after proofing.

Cacciotta - A type of cheese, its name derived from the Tuscan cacciola indicating a range of cheeses produced in the central regions of Italy from the milk of cows, sheep, goats or water buffalo. Cacciotta cheeses are cylindrical and weigh up to a kilo. The period of ripening is brief and the soft, yellow rind surrounds a white, or yellowish body, soft in texture and mild in flavor. Both artisanal and industrial production are common.

Comté - Comté (Gruyère de Comté) is a French cheese made from unpasteurized cow's milk in the Franche-Comté region of eastern Franc. The rind is a dusty-brown and the internal pâte is a pale creamy yellow. Its texture is relatively hard and flexible, with a strong and slightly sweet taste.

Cremini - A table mushroom. Point of fact, most table mushrooms are of the same variety: *Agaricus bisporus.* This variety includes portobello, cremini and the ubiquitous white button mushrooms. The difference between them is measured in age. White button mushrooms are the youngest, while portobello is the most mature, essentially an overgrown white mushroom left to grow until its button has spread into a a broad expanse of a cap. The cremini mushroom, in between a white and portobello, is a moderately mature version of the white button mushroom, boasting a browner color, firmer texture and more pronounced flavor than the younger white mushrooms. Sometimes called baby bella.

Dijon mustard - Dijon mustard dates back to 1865 when Jean Naigeon, experimenting with the traditional recipe of mustard, substituted *verjuice* (vertjus - the acidic juice of unripe grapes) for vinegar. Burgundy wine and white wine are also mixed into Dijon mustard. For the record, there are three main types of mustard in in France. Dijon is light in color, but fairly strong in flavor. Bordeaux is darker, with a milder, but more vinegary flavor, and includes sugar and usually tarragon, while Meaux mustard, with its mild flavor, is made from crushed mustard seeds instead of ground seed,

Emmentaler - Emmentaler, or Emmental, is a yellow, medium-hard Swiss cheese with a savory, slightly nutty, but mild taste. It originated in the area around Emmental, Canton Bern. It features the characteristic holes of typical of Swiss cheese. Because it melts so readily, Emmental is frequently used in sauces, grilled sandwiches and fondue,

EVOO – The acronym for Extra Virgin Olive Oil.

Frank's RedHot - is a hot sauce made from a variety of cayenne peppers. It is the primary ingredient in the first buffalo wing sauce, concocted in 1964 by Teressa Bellissimo at the Anchor Bar and Grill in Buffalo, New York. A blend of vinegar, garlic and cayenne peppers, the original Frank's RedHot ranks low on the Scoville scale with 450 SHUs, but the XTRA Hot boasts 2,000 SHUs.

Gorgonzola dolce - Also known as Gorgonzola Cremificato, this blue cheese from Lombardia, Italy, is smooth and creamy in texture. It is moister than Stilton and more buttery than Roquefort, the result of a higher moisture content and a larger curd. Made from cow's milk, it features a thin, fragile rind with white. pale yellow paste streaked with greenish-blue vein. Mild and relatively sweet tasting, with a rich and grassy aroma, it's the younger version of aged Gorgonzola and is much beloved for its soft, spreadable texture.

Greasy spoon - Since at least 1902, Greasy Spoon has been a colloquial term for a small, cheap restaurant, or diner, typically specializing in fried foods. Originally a disparaging term, a recent wave of nostalgia has elevated the status of greasy spoons so the term is now used as an endearing figure of speech.

Ground Chuck - Although any type of beef cut may be used to produce ground beef, chuck steak is a popular choice because of its richness of flavor and balance of meat-to-fat ratio. Round steak is also often used. Ground beef is usually subdivided based on the cut and fat percentage:
Chuck: 78–84% lean
Round: 85–89% lean
Sirloin: 90–95% lean

Gruyere - Gruyere is a hard, yellow, Swiss cheese, named after the town of Gruyères in Switzerland. French Gruyère style cheeses include Comté and Beaufort. Gruyère tastes sweet, but slightly salty, with a flavor that varies widely with age. It's creamy and nutty when young, becoming more assertive, earthy, and complex as it matures. When fully aged (five months to a year) it tends to have small cracks which impart a slightly grainy texture. Gruyère-style cheeses are also produced in the United States, Wisconsin having the largest production.

Harissa - Is a powerfully hot North African hot chili pepper paste. Its main ingredients include roasted red peppers, Baklouti pepper, Serrano peppers and other hot chili peppers and spices and herbs such as: Garlic paste, coriander seed, saffron, rose or caraway as well as vegetable or olive oil for preservation.

Hoisin sauce - Hoisin sauce is a thick, pungent sauce commonly used in Chinese cuisine as a glaze for meat, in addition to stir fries, or as dipping sauce. It is darkly colored in appearance and sweet and salty in taste. Although regional variants exist, hoisin sauce usually includes soy beans, red chile peppers and garlic. Also commonly added are vinegar, Chinese five spice and sugar. The word *hoisin* is Chinese for seafood, but the sauce does not contain any seafood ingredients.

Jalapeño - is a medium-sized chili pepper pod type cultivar of the species Capsicum annuum. It is of mild to medium pungency, having a range of 1,000 to 20,000 Seville units, depending on cultivar. Commonly picked and consumed while still green, it is occasionally allowed to fully ripen and turn red, orange or yellow. It is milder than the similar Serrano pepper

Jarlsberg - is a mild, cow's milk cheese populated by large, regular holes. Although it originated in Jarlsberg, Norway, it is also produced in Ohio and Ireland under licenses from Norwegian dairy producers. Jarlsberg has a yellow-wax rind and a semi-firm yellow interior with a creamy supple texture. An all-purpose cheese, used for both cooking and snacking, its flavor is mild and buttery and described as clean and rich, with a slightly sweet and nutty taste.

Kimchi - Also spelled kimchee or gimchi, *Kimchi* is Korea's national dish. Made of vegetables with a variety of seasonings, in traditional preparations, kimchi is stored underground in jars to keep the fermentation cool but unfrozen. There are hundreds of varieties of kimchi made with napa cabbage, radish, scallion, garlic, ginger or cucumber as the main ingredients. Cabbage is the most common ingredient.

Kombu – Edible kelp. Renowned as the king of seaweed.

Manchego cheese - Manchego (queso manchego) cheese is made in the La Mancha region of Spain from the milk of sheep of the Manchega breed. Official Manchego cheese is required to be aged for between 60 days and two years. Manchego has a firm and compact consistency and a buttery texture, and often contains small, unevenly distributed air pockets. The color of Manchego varies from white to ivory-yellow, and its inedible rind from yellow to brownish-beige. The cheese boasts a distinctive flavor, well-developed but not too strong, creamy with a slight piquancy, and leaves an aftertaste characteristic of sheep's milk.

McIntosh - The McIntosh Red, colloquially known as the Mac, is an apple cultivar with red and green skin, tart flavor and tender white flesh, which ripens in late September. It's considered an all-purpose apple, suitable both for cooking and eating raw.

Monterey Jack - Sometimes abbreviated as Jack cheese, is an American semi-hard cheese, customarily white made with cow's milk. It is commonly sold by itself, or mixed with Colby to make a marbled cheese known as Colby-Jack (or Co-Jack).

Meaux mustard sauce - Moutarde de Meaux, or Meaux Mustard, is made of mustard seeds (sinapis nigra/black mustard), mustard seed coat and spices crushed with water, vinegar and aromatics. The whole mustard grain is kept intact. A gourmet mustard, the recipe is a Pommery family secret with its origin dating back to antiquity. Always chill mustard. Keep it cold, it will stay hot.

Pancetta - Pancetta is an Italian bacon made of pork belly, salt cured and spiced with black pepper and sometimes other spices. In Italy, Pancetta is commonly served as a cold cut, sliced thin and eaten raw. For cooking, it is often cut into cubes.

Parmigiano-Reggiano - or Parmesan cheese, is a hard, granular cheese. The name Parmesan is often used generically for various simulations of this cheese. It has been called the King of Cheeses.

Passata - Passata is uncooked, crushed and sieved, high quality, ripe tomatoes, a formula that results in a flavorful tomato base superior to standard canned tomatoes. Passata is an excellent base for sauces and perfect as a pizza sauce.

Prosciutto - is Italian dry-cured ham, usually thinly sliced and served uncooked and called *prosciutto crudo* in Italian (or simply crudo) as distinguished from cooked ham, which is called *prosciutto cotto*.

Sambal oelek - Sambal is a hot sauce typically made from a mixture of a variety of chili peppers with secondary ingredients such as shrimp paste, fish sauce, garlic, ginger, shallot, scallion, palm sugar, lime juice, and rice vinegar or other vinegars. Sambal is native to the cuisines of Indonesia, Malaysia, Sri Lanka, Brunei and Singapore.

Serrano pepper - The Serrano pepper (Capsicum annuum) is a type of chili pepper that originated in the mountainous regions of the Mexican states of Puebla and Hidalgo. Its name is a reference to the mountains (*sierras)* of these regions. The Scoville rating of the Serrano pepper is 10,000 to 25,000 SHU. Typically eaten raw, Serranos have a bright and biting flavor notably hotter than the jalapeño pepper. Serrano peppers are commonly used in making of *pico de gallo* and salsa, as the chili is particularly fleshy compared to others, making it ideal for such dishes.

Skillet - A cast iron, or enameled cast iron, frying pan that can be placed inside of a hot oven without damaging the handle.

Slider - Slider is an American term for a small sandwich, primarily referring to small hamburgers, but can also cover any small sandwich served on a slider roll (two inch diameter) . The origin of the term is unknown, although their similarity to slider turtles resting on floating logs is noted. White Castle trademarked the spelling variant Slyder and used it between 1985 and 2009. Sliders are served as an *hors d'oeuvres*, appetizers, or *entrée*.

Speck - Speck is an English word meaning animal fat. In German, it has the same meaning, but more particularly refers to pork fat with, or without, some meat in it. Normal English usage refers to German culinary uses of smoked or pickled pork belly.

Stilton. - Stilton is a semi-soft, crumbly, English cheese produced in two varieties: Blue, renowned for its characteristically strong smell and taste, and the lesser-known White. Blue Stilton boasts blue veins radiating from its center. It melts and crumbles easily and is one of the few cheeses that freezes well.

Toast - The word toast comes from *torrere*, a Latin word that means to burn, which in contemporary English means sliced bread singed by heat. From experience you already know buttered,toasted hamburger buns, dropped, invariably land butter-side to the floor. So it goes.

Umami – Is a savory flavor, one of the five basic tastes (sweetness, sourness, bitterness, and saltiness). A Japanese loanword, *umami* translates as pleasant savory taste. Derived from the Japanese word *umai,* meaning delicious. One can home brew Umami dust with a spice grinder. Pulse 3 tablespoons bonito flakes, ½ ounce crumbled dried kombu, and ½ ounce dried shitake mushrooms into a powder. Keep in a sealed jar at room temperature for up to 2 months. Makes 2 ½ ounces.

Vidalia onion - A sweet onion variety grown in a the U. S. state of Georgia. The different varieties are unusually sweet, due to the low amount of sulfur in the soil around Vidalia, Georgia where the onions are grown.

WORCESTERSHIRE SAUCE - Complex and unique in its flavor and aroma, is a fermented liquid condiment of complex mixture created in the 1830s by Worcester chemists John Wheeley Lea and William Henry Perrins. At first blush, when Lea & Perrins concocted the recipe, the pair didn't like its pungent flavor. So they set it aside and promptly forgot about it . Months later the revisited it and discovered the taste had mellowed into what is now famously known as Worcestershire sauce. These days the sauce matures for 18 months before being blended and bottled in Worcester, England. The exact recipe is still a closely-guarded secret. Ingredients are believed to include Barley, Malt Vinegar, Spirit Vinegar, Molasses, Sugar, Salt, Anchovies, Tamarind Extract, Onions, Garlic, Spice,with flavorings of soy sauce, lemons, pickles and peppers.

Made in the USA
Middletown, DE
12 December 2022

18307560R00068